JESUS AND THE TRINITY

JESUS
AND THE TRINITY

WALTER RUSSELL BOWIE

ABINGDON PRESS
NEW YORK - NASHVILLE

TO
PAUL SOREL

Friend and Critic
the more helpful because
he speaks the layman's mind

My cordial thanks are rendered to these scholarly friends who made helpful suggestions when this book was in manuscript—Charles W. Gilkey, Holt H. Graham, Albert T. Mollegen, and Charles P. Price; and to Bettye Burke who typed it.

CONTENTS

I. WHERE THE INQUIRY BEGINS 9

II. THE CENTER OF THE DISCIPLES' FAITH 17

III. ENLARGING CONCEPTIONS OF A SAVIOR 26

IV. PAUL'S EXPERIENCE OF THE LIVING CHRIST 33

V. JOHN'S WITNESS TO THE INCARNATE WORD 43

VI. THE HOLY SPIRIT 52

VII. ATTEMPTED EXPLANATIONS OF THE FAITH 68

VIII. THE NICENE CREED 81

IX. LIVING CONSEQUENCES OF THE CREED 97

X. THE DOCTRINE OF THE TRINITY EMERGES 112

XI. DIFFICULTIES IN THE DOCTRINE 123

XII. SOME MODERN INTERPRETATIONS 137

XIII. WHEN THE DOCTRINE ENDS IN DEDICATION...... 147

INDEX 157

I

WHERE THE INQUIRY BEGINS

WHY IS THIS BOOK WRITTEN?

For a double reason: because of the everlasting urge of the mind to seek light on a great theological conception; and, deeper and more important, because of the need of every soul for life in God.

Numberless men and women who suppose that explicit theology is something they are not concerned with know well enough the need they do have. They are confused and restless, and they want to find a pattern which will put the pieces of life together in a way that makes some ultimate sense. A man may look at what he has and think that he ought to be satisfied, but he is not. He may have enough to live on, a home, a family, friends of a sort, a position to occupy; but what does it all add up to? What is he supposed to be, and what is the meaning of it all? He does not know, and his wife, for her part, may not know either In a dim way they may realize that God might be the answer, but "God" may seem only a word; and as for "the Trinity," what is that but an unintelligible phrase?

Nevertheless, great theology may open the road along which every actual person may move toward self-discovery and fulfillment. If that be so, then there is incentive enough to listen to what the deepest Christian thought has had to say concerning the richness and the relevance of God. That, then, is why this book is written: to deal with a reality so profound that it has always claimed hard thinking, but so immediate that it touches every human being, learned or unlearned, at the center of immediate concern.

Yet, it might be asked, is not the conception of a Trinity in God more a difficulty than an inspiration? Sincere Christians who sit in the pews of churches certainly do ask that in their inner thoughts even though they may not have occasion to say so out loud. Nor is it only the laymen and lay women who are concerned. Many men in the ministry actually are uneasy when they think about the Trinity. They have listened to teaching about it in the seminaries; they recognize it as something they are supposed to interpret; and if their churches follow the ancient liturgical calendar which includes "Trinity Sunday," they may feel constrained to preach on the doctrine of the Trinity once a year. But the likelihood is that they do so uncomfortably and wonder when they have finished whether they have said anything that will give people a more living faith.

The difficulty is evident enough. A doctrine which affirms that there are three Persons in God, and yet that God is one, must often bewilder the mind in the effort to find a conceptual framework in which that seeming contradiction can be enclosed. In the stress of this intellectual effort one may sometimes begin to feel that the doctrine itself has been an arbitrary speculation—the product of minds that liked to play with abstruse formulas, and in so doing turned the road of would-be Christian faith into a baffling labyrinth. Did the individual thinkers and the church councils which framed the doctrine of the Trinity have any instinctive kinship with the average person's religious

10

needs? Or were they living in a world of abtractions which must always seem irrelevant and remote?

To that question the temptation might be to answer yes. But certainly that answer would be wrong. The great leaders in the Church's thought from whom the doctrine of the Trinity has come were not only learned minds, they were also human souls. They felt, as men and women in every generation do, the pressure of life. They, like the rest of us, had need of God, and that is why they were reaching up to try to understand him. What they said, therefore, in their theology had a religious reality which we must be sensitive to recapture. Some of the words they used may have become archaic, and so it is right to ·analyze their language and to ask whether it may need to be rephrased for contemporary minds. But the important thing is to try to recognize and respond to what they meant. If we can do this, we may find the inspiration in the doctrine of the Trinity.

To find again that inspiration, we need to begin with the Inspirer. That is the reason for the title of this book: *Jesus and the Trinity*. It would be possible to begin with the doctrine of the Trinity as a finished formulation and then try to explain and justify it. But we are closer to the dynamic fact when we begin, not with a formulation, but with the living Figure by whom men were stirred to their ever-enlarging effort to interpret the wonder of what he was.

To think of Jesus is to think of that which is warm and vivid. Emotion kindles toward a person, not to unattached ideas. To remember Jesus is to remember the Master who moved in the real world among real people, who was loved and also hated, who followed his sure purpose on a steady road from the quiet of the Galilean hills to a tragic climax in Jerusalem, who died on

11

a Roman cross and prayed for those who brought him there, "Father, forgive them, for they know not what they do." Jesus himself has always been at the heart of Christian devotion. This fact echoes in Christian hymns from many centuries. "Jesus, thou Joy of loving hearts"; "Jesus, my Lord, my God, my all"; "Jesus, the very thought of Thee with sweetness fills the breast"; and

> When I survey the wondrous cross
> Where the young Prince of glory died,
> My richest gain I count but loss,
> And pour contempt on all my pride.

The unlearned and the simplehearted, who have little knowledge of developed theology, may feel the reality of Jesus as a power that lays hold of their minds and hearts.

Why then, it is sometimes asked and argued, is there need to move beyond that? When we go on to speak of "Jesus *and* the Trinity," what can happen except to be led into a dim region of speculation, abstract and unreal?

Yet as a matter of fact every awareness of Jesus must lead sooner or later to larger thinking. In the actual history of the Christian Church, remembrance of Jesus has always waked a wondering about him which grew inevitably into questions and answers as to how he was related to the infinite Reality of God.

The key to the distinctive nature of theology is found in its own proper source, the reality we call Jesus Christ. Christians think about the meaning of life not on the basis of abstract ideas alone, nor on the basis of experience in general; but from the standpoint of this one strand of history where we believe life is so broken open for us that we can see into its depth more than we can anywhere else. We never exhaust the meaning of Jesus Christ.[1]

It is the fact of Jesus' life and death, plus the interpretation of it, that makes the fullness of Christian faith. As Paul Tillich has written:

> Christianity is what it is through the affirmation that Jesus of Nazareth, who has been called "the Christ," is actually the Christ, namely, he who brings the new state of things, the New Being. . . . Jesus as the Christ is both a historical fact and a subject of believing reception. . . . If there were no personal life in which existential estrangement had been overcome, the New Being would have remained a quest and an expectation and would not be a reality in time and space. . . . Nevertheless, the other side, the believing reception of Jesus *as* the Christ, calls for equal emphasis. . . . The receptive side of the Christian event is as important as the factual side. And only their unity creates the event upon which Christianity is based.[2]

Thus there is vital sequence from the concrete and immediate remembrance of Jesus to the ultimate beliefs concerning him toward which Christian thinking has gone. It may be a long road from the first partial knowledge men had of the Man of Galilee to the Church's developed creeds about him, but it is a living and unbroken road. So between the first and last terms in the title of this book there is no disassociation. That which became at length the formulated "doctrine of the Trinity," like all other great theological conceptions, did not begin in academic

[1] Daniel Day Williams, *What Present Day Theologians Are Thinking* (New York: Harper & Brothers, 1959), p. 175.
[2] *Systematic Theology* (Chicago: University of Chicago Press, 1957), II, 97-99. Copyright by the University of Chicago Press and used by permission.

interests. It began with a disclosure and a discovery. In Jesus the disciples saw a magnitude of life which went beyond all ordinary explanations and descriptions. "Who do you say that I am?" the original twelve had been asked at Caesarea Philippi. From that time on, not only by what Jesus said but by their astonished experience of what he was, those who looked to him were continually confronted by that provocation to their thinking.

So in the chapters that follow there is—or there ought to be—some such element of suspense as there is in a developing drama. The climax does not appear at the beginning. It must be led up to by stages, each of which approaches nearer to the as-yet-not-seen fulfillment to which they all converge. Thus, not until nine chapters have preceded it can there come the chapter that may rightly be entitled, "The Doctrine of the Trinity Emerges." But the significance of each chapter before that lies in some special reflection of the impact of Jesus upon the minds of men who loved him, out of which at length the conception of the Trinity would grow.

The interpretations in the New Testament and in the early Church of Jesus and his relationship to the infinite God were fragmentary and gradual. What Peter said in his preaching in Jerusalem, as recorded in the book of Acts, was not what Paul would presently say in his letters to the Romans and the Colossians. And what Paul said would be followed by the great conceptions embodied in the prologue, and in all the subsequent portrayal of Jesus, in the Fourth Gospel. Various threads were being woven toward what was being sought for: a pattern of thinking which might fully express the reality of Jesus, human and divine.

At length the Church, at the Councils of Nicea, of Constantinople, and of Chalcedon in the fourth and fifth centuries, arrived at the pattern which it believed to express, as far as human words could do so, the ultimate truth concerning Jesus and the nature of God revealed in him. It declared its faith that there is "one God the Father Almighty, Maker of heaven and earth"; that Jesus, who was born and lived among men and was crucified and rose again, was and is "the only-begotten Son of God; Begotten of his Father before all worlds, God of God, Light of Light, Very God of very God; Begotten, not made; Being of one substance with the Father; By whom all things were made"; and that in the oneness of the Godhead there is also the Holy Spirit through whom the grace of God revealed in Christ is brought home to the hearts of men redeemed. Since then the Church has been bidden to pray as in the collect for Trinity Sunday in the Book of Common Prayer, "Almighty and everlasting God, who hast given unto us thy servants grace, by the confession of a true faith, to acknowledge the glory of the eternal Trinity, and in the power of the Divine Majesty to worship the Unity; We beseech thee that thou wouldest keep us stedfast in this faith."

But the trouble for many honest minds is that they may be confronted with that statement before they are ready for it. "How can I be 'stedfast in this faith,'" they ask, "when I do not know what it means? How can faith find a firm foundation in language that leaves me in a cloudland? If I start from the vividness of Jesus, must I end in *this*?"

Concerning that genuine difficulty, what needs to be remembered is that spiritual conviction is the living and crucial thing, deeper and more abiding than any language-expression of it. In its actual experience the early Church felt itself lifted up by a power which had in itself the reality at once of Christ

15

and God and the Holy Spirit. After three or four centuries of thinking, that experience was put into words as the doctrine of the Trinity; and that doctrine has helped to convey the faith of great scholars and great saints. Yet always it is a fact that in the effort to conceive and to express the infinite truths of God no human forms of thought or language can be final. As Leonard Hodgson has rightly written:

It is not sufficient to say simply that each generation must see for itself what was seen by the original recipients of the revelation; as the years go by God enables successive generations to see both what their fathers saw and more.[3]

But the matter of first importance is that if we are ever to see more than the fathers saw we must begin by being sure that we see what they did see. It is possible that our thought may question certain aspects of traditional doctrines and express them in new terms. Whether that be true in reference to the doctrine of the Trinity—and if so, to what extent—we are yet to consider. But this is certain: our right to our convictions concerning any doctrine is subject first to our knowledge of *why* that doctrine came to be and what the eternal values are which it was trying to express. What developed into the Church's creed of a triune God did not begin with unrelated speculations. It began, as we have remembered, with the living impressions men got from Jesus, with what they said "we have heard, . . . have seen with our eyes, . . . have looked upon and touched with our hands, concerning the word of life" (I John 1:1).

We now turn directly to the New Testament.

[3] *The Doctrine of the Trinity* (New York: Charles Scribner's Sons, 1944), p. 35. Used by permission of the publisher and James Nisbet and Company Limited.

II

THE CENTER
OF THE DISCIPLES' FAITH

IN THE NEW TESTAMENT THERE ARE NO SUCH WORDS AS "THE Trinity." But there is much about God the Father, about Jesus, who is called the Son, and about a Holy Spirit.

Back of the New Testament is the Old Testament. The world did not have to wait till the Christian era to discover God. For the people of Israel, more than for any other people of the earth, God was the conscious center of their life. Their thought of him had grown through many centuries—grown from the naïve conceptions of a primitive folk to the noble faith to which seers and prophets had lighted the way. God, who may have been seen first as the mysterious power investing great trees or springs or rocks with a dread sacredness, or coming down in terror through the thunderclouds of Sinai, became the God of the Ten Commandments and of the moral law by which the people now were bound to him. God, who had been thought of as a tribal deity, the God of battles whose prestige was bound up with the fortunes of his particular people, became in the illumined conscience of an Amos the judge of all the peoples of the earth. Elijah proclaimed his will for righteousness; Isaiah bowed down before his holiness; Hosea, out of his own sufferings, rose to his inspired vision of God as redeeming love.

Among any people crude and primitive elements in religion will always linger here and there; and this, of course, was still true in Jesus' time. But there were great souls who in thought and will were reaching up continually to the Holy One; and to simple men and women also God was in the framework of their daily lives. Fishermen by the Lake of Galilee, the Peters and the Andrews, the Jameses and the Johns, did not need someone to rouse them out of unbelief. In their blood and training was the consciousness of the everlasting God to whom they were accountable.

Then came Jesus. Two of the Gospels tell that he had been born by a heavenly miracle of a virgin. However we may interpret those accounts, it is clear that the men who encountered Jesus had never heard of them. They saw Jesus as a man among men, fascinating and compelling. In his notable little book, *The Man Christ Jesus,* John Knox has made vivid the impression Jesus must have created and the qualities which drew fishermen and others of their virile sort to follow him.

"Greatness," writes Matthew Arnold, . . . "is a spiritual condition worthy to excite love, interest, and admiration; and the outward proof of possessing greatness is that we excite love, interest and admiration." One finds here the crowning proof of Jesus' greatness—a proof in the last resort far more convincing than anything in the Gospels. Indeed, the Gospels themselves are most significant not for their particular contents, but as being themselves witnesses to the "love, interest and admiration" with which Jesus was regarded from the beginning.[1]

It was a tense time in Israel. The yoke of Roman dominion lay heavy on the people and there was restlessness everywhere

[1] *The Man Christ Jesus* (Chicago: Willett, Clark & Co., 1941), p. 26.

—the restlessness of angry resentment against conditions without, and the inner trouble of the more spiritually sensitive who felt the everlasting conflict between God's purpose for them and their own sins and shortcomings. Since the time of the great prophets, seven hundred years before, there had burned in the nation the hope that the Messiah would come. The concepts of what the Messiah would be and of the way in which he would appear varied like the shapes of wind-blown flame. In the expectation of many, the Messiah would be a mighty conqueror, clothed with the terrible vengeance of the Lord, to be the deliverer of God's people and the instrument of his punishment upon the oppressors under whom they had suffered too long. Now and then some figure would arise, like Judas of Galilee in the years of Jesus' boyhood, who dared rebellion against Rome; and always there was the possibility that one of these men might draw to himself not only the instinctive patriotism, but also the desperate passion of Israel's religious hope. There could be "false Messiahs," and actually it was to come to pass that one who did claim to be Messiah, Bencosiba, would lead the catastrophic ultimate defiance of the Roman power that was smashed by the legions of Hadrian in the second century and ended, after a frightful siege, in the merciless destruction of Jerusalem.

In the expectation of others Messiah would come, not necessarily in war, but in some other course of this world's events that would be nonetheless decisive. He would be the anointed of the Lord who should rule a people once more restored to freedom. Was it not written in the psalms, "Why do the heathen rage, and the people imagine a vain thing? The kings of the earth set themselves, and the rulers take counsel together. . . . Yet have I set my king upon my holy hill of Zion. . . . Ask of me, and I shall give thee the heathen for thine inheritance, and the utter-

19

most parts of the earth for thy possession" (Ps. 2:1, 2, 6, 8 K.J.V.). So the crowd on Palm Sunday could cry: "Hosanna to the Son of David! Blessed be he who comes in the name of the Lord!" (Matt. 21:9).

But there were others, perhaps a larger number, who thought of the coming of Messiah in a more unearthly way. Although the hot blood of some might rouse them to desperate devices, the majority began to recognize that any successful revolt against Rome was only a fanatical illusion. The glories of David's kingdom—which imagination had magnified in wistful retrospect—were not likely to be brought back by any human means. So the thought of Israel in the century before and after the time of the birth of Jesus had become increasingly apocalyptic. Men turned to the mystical prophecy of the book of Daniel. Through its symbolism they recognized the description of the evil powers of the present world and then came to these tremendous promises:

I beheld till the thrones were cast down, and the Ancient of days did sit, whose garment was white as snow, and the hair of his head like the pure wool: his throne was like the fiery flame, and his wheels as burning fire. . . . I saw in the night visions, and, behold, one like the Son of man came with the clouds of heaven, and came to the Ancient of days, and they brought him near before him. And there was given him dominion, and glory, and a kingdom, that all people, nations, and languages, should serve him: his dominion is an everlasting dominion, which shall not pass away, and his kingdom that which shall not be destroyed."—Dan. 7:9, 13, 14. (K.J.V.)

Against the background of that sort of thinking the figure of Jesus moves, as the Gospels make him visible. What men felt about him was necessarily affected by the thought-forms of their time. When he began to wake their admiration and provoke their speculation, they turned to the conceptions which were immediately familiar as they tried to explain his greatness. The crowd regarded him as another in the mighty succession of the prophets. The superstitious said that he might be not merely *a* prophet, but the awesome John the Baptist risen from the dead. But Simon Peter's impulsive mind broke through to a new dimension: "You are the Christ!" he exclaimed at Caesarea Philippi (Mark 8:29).

What he meant then was a long way off from the conception of Christ as the eternal Son, the second person of the Trinity, which would be a part of the Church's ultimate creed. "The Christ" probably stood in Peter's mind for what it meant in the general mind: the long hoped-for Messiah who would fulfill the popular expectation of a deliverer come with conquering power. That this *is* what he was thinking seems to be evidenced by his outspoken horror when he heard Jesus indicate that instead of his ministry being one of obvious triumph, it would culminate in his going up to Jerusalem to suffer and to die. Moreover, the idea which the other disciples held appears to have been shaped by the same hope that the crowd mind cherished concerning the Messiah. So James and John came to Jesus one day with their particular persuasion:

"We want you to do for us whatever we ask of you." And he said to them, "What do you want me to do for you?" And they said to him, "Grant us to sit, one at your right hand and one at your left, in your glory."—Mark 10:37

The Gospel of Luke, in the story of the two disciples going back from Jerusalem to Emmaus after the Crucifixion, has them say, "We had hoped that he was the one to redeem Israel"

21

(24:21). According to the book of Acts, even after the Resurrection, the disciples were still asking "Lord, will you at this time restore the kingdom to Israel?" (1:6).

We are not asking yet what is the ultimate conception of Jesus that can most nearly express the fullness of his reality. That is, of course, the crucial question, on which we shall say more hereafter. Our initial need is simpler: it is to try to understand what his disciples understood—or thought they understood—for it was out of *this* that the ultimate declarations and doctrines of the Church would begin to grow. Apparently, up to the time of the Crucifixion, their thought had hardly begun to break beyond the chrysalis of the great, yet distinctively Jewish, hope that here might be the Messiah who would bring dramatic deliverance to the chosen people.

The Crucifixion was a catastrophic shock. It left the disciples disorganized and dismayed. Where was the hope of a victorious Messiah now? The whole world of their expectations had disintegrated into dust.

Then came the amazing morning of the Resurrection, the breathless word of the women who went early to the garden tomb and found the body of their Master gone; the appearance of the risen Jesus to Mary Magdalene in the garden, to Peter, to the two disciples on the Emmaus road, then to all the disciples in the Upper Room. The accounts of the Resurrection in the four Gospels quiver with an excitement which belongs to an experience so ineffable that it could not be described in one cool and consistent picture of what the disciples saw and heard. But the reality of their experience of a risen Lord, and the effect upon them, was tremendous and transforming. Now they were sure that not less, but more, than they had ever believed about the greatness of Jesus was true. How, then, should they interpret him and declare him in Jerusalem?

The first evidence that comes to us of their answer to that is in the early tradition embodied in the book of Acts of Peter's preaching on the day of Pentecost.

Men of Israel, hear these words: Jesus of Nazareth, a man attested to you by God with mighty works and wonders and signs which God did through him in your midst, as you yourselves know —this Jesus delivered up according to the definite plan and foreknowledge of God, you crucified and killed by the hands of lawless men. But God raised him up, having loosed the pangs of death, because it was not possible for him to be held by it. . . . Let all the house of Israel therefore know assuredly that God has made him both Lord and Christ, this Jesus whom you crucified.—Acts 2:22-24

And at the gate of the temple not long afterward he preached of how "The God of Abraham and of Isaac and of Jacob, the God of our fathers, glorified his servant Jesus, whom you delivered up and denied" (Acts 3:13) and who yet, notwithstanding that denial, was now recalled as "the Author of life, whom God raised from the dead." Then Peter went on:

What God foretold by the mouth of all the prophets that his Christ should suffer, he thus fulfilled. Repent therefore, and turn again, that your sins may be blotted out, that times of refreshing may come from the presence of the Lord, and that he may send the Christ appointed for you, Jesus, whom heaven must receive until the time for establishing all that God spoke by the mouth of his holy prophets from of old.—Acts 3:18-21

Here was a different conception from that which Peter had had when he cried out his confession at Caesarea Philippi. When he said then, "You are the Christ!" he may well have believed

23

that Jesus as Messiah would be the immediate deliverer for whom the crowd, with its patriotic passion, was looking. Certainly he had no conception then that the Messiah would suffer and die. Now his thought had moved forward into the dimension of the apocalyptic hope. Jesus who had been crucified was alive in God. He would come again, this time from heaven in manifest and conquering glory. The great thing was to be ready for that coming.

This apparently was the expectation that dominated the thought of the Christian Church in the first generation. It would be reflected in the earliest letter written by the apostle Paul— that to the Thessalonians about the middle of the century.

We would not have you ignorant, brethren, concerning those who are asleep, that you may not grieve as others do who have no hope. For since we believe that Jesus died and rose again, even so, through Jesus, God will bring with him those who have fallen asleep. For this we declare to you by the word of the Lord, that we who are alive, who are left until the coming of the Lord, shall not precede those who have fallen asleep. For the Lord himself will descend from heaven with a cry of command, with the archangel's call, and with the sound of the trumpet of God. And the dead in Christ will rise first; then we who are alive, who are left, shall be caught up together with them in the clouds to meet the Lord in the air; and so shall we always be with the Lord.—I Thess. 4:13-17

This vivid and dramatic return of the Lord did not come. Undoubtedly there was wistful disappointment. Some were asking "Where is the promise of his coming? For ever since the fathers fell asleep, all things have continued as they were from the beginning of creation" (II Pet. 3:4). It began to appear that the reality of Jesus as Christ and Lord would not fit into the

24

traditional anticipation of a son of David who would restore his earthly kingdom, or of an apocalyptic figure whose Second Coming in visible glory might occur at any hour.

But meanwhile something else was happening. Within the framework of the hope that something tremendous would issue from the heavens there grew the realization that already something transfiguring was happening in men's hearts. As the first epistle of Peter expressed it:

Blessed be the God and Father of our Lord Jesus Christ! By his great mercy we have been born anew to a living hope through the resurrection of Jesus Christ from the dead. . . . Without having seen him you love him; though you do not now see him you believe in him and rejoice with unutterable and exalted joy. As the outcome of your faith you obtain the salvation of your souls.—I Pet. 1:3, 8, 9

Words like those were the reflection of an expanding fact. For the disciples of Jesus life had assumed a new dimension. It was no longer a matter of waiting for something dramatic to occur tomorrow; in a deep spiritual sense Christ was a power in their midst already. They were being made into new persons in their confidence, their courage, and their strength. A realization was dawning on them of the relationship of Jesus to an eternal presence of God, of which they were aware through their faith in him. By the time the Gospels should come to be written late in the first century, there would still, of course, be no developed doctrine of a Trinity; but there would be a consciousness of the limitless significance of Jesus out of which the ultimate great affirmations of Christian faith would grow.

III

ENLARGING
CONCEPTIONS OF A SAVIOR

THE HOPE FOR A MESSIAH WAS BORN OUT OF THE DEEP RELIGIOUS longings of the great prophets. To them God was the supreme reality. For God's will to become sovereign among his people, sovereign in their own hearts and in the hearts of all men everywhere—that was what they cried out to behold. This manifestation of God might bring changes in outward conditions, but what mattered most was that there should be a quickening of men's souls. Isaiah's description of what he experienced in the temple is the symbol of what the great religious spirits sought for: a vision of God "high and lifted up," the voices of seraphim crying, "Holy, holy, holy is the Lord of hosts," the bringing by the seraph messenger of the live coal from God's altar to touch the unclean human lips, and the promise, "Lo, this hath touched thy lips; and thine iniquity is taken away, and thy sin purged" (Isa. 6:1-7 K.J.V.).

But in the actuality of life the heavenly vision always becomes mixed with the influences of earth. People might want God's salvation, but it was easier and more instinctive to want it on the level of their own desires. If God's power was to be manifest, let it be shown most evidently in the destruction of their enemies, the amelioration of their lot, the enhancement of their prosperity. That is the way Israel—like any other people—was tempted to interpret the covenant with God. So the conception of Messiah, and of what he would come to do, began to be seen through the distorting smoke of earthiness. It had been prophesied (Isa. 11:5) that "righteousness shall be the girdle of his waist, and faithfulness the girdle of his loins." But "righteousness" could mean the setting of things in order according to what human pride (thinking itself always to be religious passion) should consider to be proper. Therefore the mission of Messiah could be interpreted more and more in terms not so much of spiritual hunger as of selfishness disguised as pious hope. The penetrating mind of Jesus saw that unerringly. If the people, unprepared, began to hear and spread the rumor that he had come to be Messiah, their expectations would begin to run in their own instinctive channel. They would come to him "for the loaves and fishes"—for immediate benefits or for the satisfaction of their nationalistic hopes. Therefore, when Peter had cried out, "You are the Christ," the immediate record of the Gospel is that Jesus "charged them to tell no one about him" (Mark 8:30). When it did become evident to the crowd that whatever Jesus might be, he was not the kind of deliverer they most wanted, many of those who had at first been attracted to him, "drew back and no longer went about with him" (John 6:66). Also it may well have been for this same reason that the original attachment of Judas turned into sullen disappointment and at last into betrayal. A Messiah who gave no exciting signs of power in the realm where men's earthly ambitions moved— was *this* a Messiah worth being concerned about?

Yet always there was the deeper spiritual understanding waiting to break through. Here and there were men like old Simeon, "righteous and devout, looking for the consolation of Israel" (Luke 2:25). And Peter, John, and others of the twelve were capable of a spiritual understanding. Although they were slow

27

JESUS AND THE TRINITY

to learn, they would understand at length what the saviorhood of Jesus meant as an inner redeeming fact.

But there needed to be a still greater understanding and interpretation. These came—in the apostle Paul.

Paul lived and moved habitually—as some men move uncertainly and now-and-then—in the compelling orbit of the consciousness of God. To feel himself at one with the will of God, his ways made sure in that divine control—this was what he longed for. His early years had gone by and he had not found it. His tremendous moral earnestness was to him more of a scourge than an inspiration. Along with desire for goodness went always his sense of the terrible reality of evil—evil in the world, evil creeping insidiously into his own mind and heart with its subtle corruption of even his highest impulses. Like that great figure who would appear in a century nearer our own, Martin Luther, who was so immeasurably influenced by the apostle and in essential ways so like him, Paul suffered the torment of inner conflict and division. Often he despaired of ever finding peace.

I find it to be a law, that when I want to do right, evil lies close at hand. For I delight in the law of God, in my inmost self, but I see in my members another law at war with the law of my mind and making me captive to the law of sin which dwells in my members. Wretched man that I am! Who will deliver me from this body of death?—Rom. 7:21-24

The story of how he sought deliverance can be read in part in the book of Acts and in the poignant references in Paul's own letters. All his life he had been taught, and he believed intensely, that God had revealed his will for his people in the law—the law that had been given as part of Israel's covenant to Moses, and that had been interpreted and made explicit by

28

the teaching of devoted scribes and rabbis through all the following centuries. If he could keep that law, he would be within the circle of salvation. If he could obey it truly, then his divided self could find its peace.

But he could not keep the law. He might observe its outward precepts, but how could he control his imagination and his desires? What did it avail him to keep himself from overt acts of evil, if all the while evil was infecting his central self? The law which was meant to deliver him from sin made him all the more conscious of his sinfulness, because its prohibitions kept throwing their accusing light on the impulses within which he could not prevent. He wrote:

I should not have known what it is to covet, if the law had not said, "You shall not covet." But sin, finding opportunity in the commandment, wrought in me all kinds of covetousness. . . . The very commandment which promised life proved to be death to me.
—Rom. 7:7-8, 10

Covetousness, sensual desire, pride, all the secret and invisible sins—how could he ever get rid of these? And not being rid of them, how could he escape the judgment of God?

It is not always easy to realize how close that conflict of Paul comes to our own concern. Paul may seem a long way off in time and in the level above ordinary human understanding on which we assume he must have moved. He is a figure so classic as to be necessarily remote, we think, from familiar comparisons, up somewhere on a cloudy stage where the action and the language are such that only those learned in theological abstractions can understand him. It is true, of course, that Paul was a great genius, and therefore different in degree from our ordinary selves, and it is true also that he was far more explicitly conscious

29

of a need for God than are the rank and file of people. But underneath those facts is the more essential fact that the need he had, which produced his agonizing inner conflict, is the same need that men have had in every age—and the same need that we have now. It is to get the inner life put together; to get rid of the fears and doubts that split us into fragments; to find some certainty that pulls all our energies together; to feel and act like people who are *whole*. The New Testament is full of instances of individuals who were torn apart inside, like the wild man among the tombs in Gadara who said his name was "Legion." Back of the first century language of "evil spirits" and "possession by demons" we can recognize the everlastingly contemporary fact of split personality, which only in extreme cases becomes insanity but which in thousands of the so-called sane means the torment of worry and hidden harassment and crippling fear. That condition of mind and spirit is what William James analyzed and illustrated as "the divided self."

How can the divided self be put together?—that is the everlasting question. We know the answer that is fashionable in our time. Go to a psychoanalyst. Dig down into the subconscious and find out at length what are the chained fears and the hidden impulses, buried like forgotten prisoners in dark dungeons, whose hollow cries have made the hitherto faint and unintelligible, but hideous, echoes which have haunted our peace. Let these be disposed of, and we shall be serene and free.

This is beautiful, if true; and there is truth in it. The technique of the analyst may help many persons to understand their problems. It may release them from old complexes which have been their torment. But the trouble is that it cannot always put an integrating purpose in their place. They may be left like the house in Jesus' parable, "swept and garnished" with the evil spirit driven out, but standing empty as an invitation for seven other spirits worse than the first to enter in (Matt. 12:43, 45).

More than a century ago, James Chalmers of Scotland preached a sermon so relevant to real people that it is lastingly remembered. It was on "The Expulsive Power of a New Affection," and his message was that the disturbances in human souls can only be disposed of when something positive and powerful comes in. That was what happened with the apostle Paul. And it is through what happened to him that we are moving forward along the not-always-referred-to but never-forgotten road of the thesis of this book: that it is not in speculative forms, but in living facts, that we can first perceive the realities which would lead at length to a formulated faith in the Triune God.

For Paul those were years in which his inner conflict became increasingly acute. His loyalty to old convictions made him cling with fiercer determination to his search for salvation through the law. If, through the promptings of the law, he could drive out the evil and the moral weakness from his life, then he would have won God's favor. All his pride as a Pharisee was committed to that belief. But meanwhile there was a challenge to it, a challenge that he hated and that he set out to destroy. It was the challenge presented by a group of people who dared to say that a man who had treated lightly the particularities of the law, who had been condemned by the authorities of Israel for his blasphemous claim to be Messiah, sentenced by a Roman governor, and hung up to die on a Roman cross—that *this* man was the Anointed sent from God. If that were true, then everything in which Israel had trusted would be shattered. What would become of the hope of victory for Israel over its enemies? What of the proud belief in a Covenant given only to a people who kept the law? These followers of Jesus represented an evil force

31

which ought to be exterminated. So Saul of Tarsus, as he was then known, went out to arrest and persecute—but with unforeseen and incredible results. He had thought that his whole personality was fused now by one unquestioning purpose. The more he hated these disciples of a blasphemer, the more he could be sure of his own rightness. But was he sure? He had stood by when the man named Stephen had been stoned to death, had seen his face "as it had been the face of an angel," and had heard his voice as he was dying, "Lord Jesus, receive my spirit" (Acts 6: 15; 7:59). He had marked also the bearing of humble men and women whom he had arrested. They seemed to have something he knew he did not have. This Jesus had somehow given them a strength he could not break and a serenity his own soul could not match. Had his search for salvation, for his own life and for the life of Israel, been on a dead-end road? His conceptions of what the Messiah must be and of the manner of his kingdom—were these all wrong? This incomprehensible Jesus whose spirit, in spite of his resistance, he had somehow seen reflected in his disciples—must he be acknowledged not only as Messiah but as the immediate savior for his own troubled soul? Between that terrific subjective tension and the objective reality that surpasses the analysis of this earth came the lightning flash of Paul's vision on the Damascus road. Here was the expulsive power of the new affection to which Paul was henceforth to be obedient, and in which obedience he would never again be a divided self.

But how could that power come to Paul through Christ? Only if in some unexampled way Christ was linked with God. The thinkers of the Church would remember that as they meditated upon the divineness of Christ, which would lead on to the conception of the Trinity.

IV

PAUL'S
EXPERIENCE OF THE LIVING CHRIST

CONVERSION, WROTE WILLIAM JAMES, IS
the process, gradual or sudden, by which a self hitherto divided and
consciously wrong inferior and unhappy, becomes unified and consciously right superior and happy, in consequence of its firmer hold
upon religious realities.[1]

That brilliant sentence is a sufficient description not only of
what happens in conversion in general, but also of what happened in the particular conversion of Saul the Pharisee and per-
secutor into the apostle Paul. Here is what was done. But that
leaves us only at the threshold of the greater question: *What
did* it? What was back of the process of Paul's conversion, and
how would he himself interpret it?

One of the uncertainties to which it would be most exciting
to have an answer is the question of whether Paul had ever
seen Jesus in the flesh. As thoughtful a scholar as W. M. Macgregor could believe that he had. "It is no unsupported phan-
tasy," Macgregor wrote, "that Paul, though with jaundiced eyes,
had seen Jesus, thinking of Him only as a disturber of the worship of God, and that the memory of the encounter had re-

[1] *The Varieties of Religious Experience* (London: Longmans, Green and
Co., 1903), p. 189.

33

mained with him, like a fragrance subtly influencing thought and memory and feeling." That, it must be recognized, does not go beyond inference and surmise. There is no concrete evidence that Paul had come face to face with Jesus before the Crucifixion; if he had done so, it would seem almost inevitable that he would have made some explicit reference to it. Be that as it may, it can hardly be believed that Paul could have failed to get some vivid impression of him. The ministry of Jesus in Galilee, which had become so widely known and disturbing that Pharisees and scribes went up from Jerusalem to watch him; the final crowded events around and in the Holy City itself—the alleluias of the crowd on the road from Bethany, the cleansing of the temple, the indignant questioning of the authorities and Jesus' answers; the arrest in Gethsemane, the trials before the Sanhedrin and before Pilate—all these were not "things done in a corner." Paul must have had his vivid mental picture of the man who was at the center of that drama. He saw him then, of course, in the distorted focus of his own hostility—saw his power as presumption, his hold upon the people as the result of heresy, his tremendous influence as a threat to respectable religion. But even from this twisted angle of appraisal he would be aware of Jesus' greatness. He could not escape his challenging significance. Then somehow—from words spread here and there, from ideas that crept into his thinking unawares, perhaps from what he saw in the face of Stephen or in humble men and women in the course of the persecution—the real Jesus began to take compelling shape for him. By the time he set out on what was to prove his fateful journey to Damascus, this real Jesus had so affected his imagination that he could recognize him and respond to him in the vision which he saw.

At this point there can come objections which must be fairly dealt with. Was there a sure relationship between the Jesus of the Gospels and the Jesus of Paul's own mystical and ecstatic experience? Some have questioned whether Paul was actually interested in the Jesus of the human contacts that the Gospels tell of. It is pointed out that after his conversion Paul did not immediately turn toward the men who had known Jesus best, did not, as he put it, "confer with flesh and blood," but went off for long solitude in Arabia, as though the knowledge given in his own revelation was enough. His vision was for him a direct and authentic revelation. The gospel he was to preach was not "man's gospel"; he had not been won to it by anybody else's persuasion, "nor was I taught it" (Gal. 1:11-13). It had come to him in a flash of heavenly illumination. He would later write to the church in Corinth: "From now on, therefore, we regard no one from a human point of view; even though we once regarded Christ from a human point of view, we regard him thus no longer" (II Cor. 5:16).

But as to the latter there is the significant commentary of James Reid:

The statement that he no longer regarded Christ from a human point of view means just what it says. All false ideas about him were gone. Gone were the prejudices that busied themselves with his lowly birth, his humble social position, his association with doubtful characters, his disregard of the law, his appeal to the ignorant and oppressed. These all disappeared when the scales fell from Paul's eyes and he saw "the glory of God in the face of Christ" (II Cor. 4:6). . . . . This does not mean, as has been suggested, that Paul was indifferent to the earthly life and teaching of Jesus, and that he depended upon the Spirit for all he knew. The guidance of the Spirit has no content for us apart from that fact in history which was the earthly life and teaching of Christ. . . . The Moravian who

35

talked with Wesley on the voyage to Georgia made this point when he asked, "Do you know Jesus?" Wesley replied, "I know that he is the Savior of the world." "Yes," rejoiced the Moravian, "but do you know him?" [2]

Although it is true that Paul did not at once go to join the original disciples after his conversion, it is to be remembered that later he did go "up to Jerusalem to visit Cephas, and remained with him fifteen days" (Gal. 1:18). What would they have talked of through fifteen days if it was not of Jesus? Surely what Peter in that time told of the Master he had followed must have both paralleled and enriched the picture which Paul's mind intuitively had already formed of him. Paul himself was afterwards to maintain with eager insistence that his perception of the risen Lord had the same complete validity as belonged to the appearances to the disciples in Jerusalem. It was the one who had come back to them who had come also to him. "Have I not seen Jesus our Lord?" (I Cor. 9:1.) "Last of all ·. . . , he appeared also to me." (I Cor. 15:8.)

When one reads Paul's letters, one can see that the Christ who had become the center of his devotion is in the likeness of the man who moves through the Gospels. Unfailingly one recognizes the quality of Jesus: his white flame of goodness, his gentleness and compassion, his unsparing judgment which yet was only the other side of his redeeming love. It has been memorably suggested about the thirteenth chapter of Paul's first letter to the Corinthians, which tells of love that "suffereth long and is kind," that "vaunteth not itself," that "beareth all things, believeth all things, hopeth all things"—"substitute the name 'Christ' for every mention of the word 'love' in this thrilling

[2] *The Interpreter's Bible* (Nashville: Abingdon Press, 1957), X, 337-38.

chapter of the epistle and in the end we have another marvelous portrait of the Master." [3]

But the significance of Jesus for Paul was greater than it could have been to those who knew him before the Crucifixion. The Jesus of Nazareth whom he had once believed to have been rightly condemned as a false messiah, he saw now as risen, alive in God, and—in spite of all his previous denial—meant to be the master of his soul. This was more than belief in Jesus as Messiah according to the traditional conception. That traditional conception, with its hope of Messiah coming in the clouds, was expressed—as we have remembered—in the sermon of Peter at Pentecost, when what he pointed forward to was this: "That times of refreshing may come from the presence of the Lord, and that he may send the Christ appointed for you, Jesus, whom the heaven must receive until the time for establishing all that God spoke by the mouth of his holy prophets from of old" (Acts 3:19-21). There were moments, as in the period of his writing to the Thessalonians, when Paul's thought reflected that same expectation. But over and above that was a more immediate awareness. Jesus as the saving Christ was not only a future hope; he was also a present fact. "The love of Christ controls us," Paul wrote to the church in Corinth (II Cor. 5:14). As he sought words strong enough to express the power of that love he cried:

I am sure that neither death, nor life, nor angels, nor principalities, nor things present, nor things to come, nor powers, nor height, nor depth, nor anything else in all creation, will be able to separate us from the love of God in Christ Jesus our Lord.—Rom. 8:38-39

[3] John Short in *The Interpreter's Bible, op. cit.*, X, 173.

"Christ Jesus has made me his own," he wrote to the Philippians (3:12). And in his letter to the Galatians he rose to the still more exalted affirmation, "It is no longer I who live, but Christ who lives in me" (2:20).

In what Paul had experienced there was a development in his thought of God that would have seemed incredible a few years before. With his Jewish inheritance and tradition, nothing was more certain for him than the awful incomparableness of God. God might speak his word and execute his will through his agents—through the prophets, through angelic messengers, through the Messiah, who also would be his servant. But for Paul more than that had come to be the truth. Jesus as the Christ went beyond the former conceptions of Messiah. He was not only the agent of God; he was part of the very life of God himself. When Paul tried to describe the saving influences which had come to him, he attributed them to God the high and lifted up, and in the next breath—and indistinguishably—to the Christ who had been made man, was crucified, and now was risen. "Grace to you and peace from God our Father and the Lord Jesus Christ." (Rom. 1:7.) "God judges the secrets of men by Christ Jesus." (Rom. 2:16.) Sinners are justified by God's grace "through the redemption which is in Christ Jesus" (Rom. 3:24). "We have peace with God through our Lord Jesus Christ." (Rom. 5:1.) "The free gift of God is eternal life in Christ Jesus our Lord." (Rom. 6:23.) "We preach . . . Christ the power of God and the wisdom of God." (I Cor. 1:23-24.) "You are Christ's and Christ is God's." (I Cor. 3:23.) "There is one God, the Father, from whom are all things and for whom we exist, and one Lord, Jesus Christ, through whom are all things and through whom we exist." (I Cor. 8:6.)

Astonishing words those were. As words they have been so

often read and heard and preached about that we may treat them as familiar and file them away in the pigeonholes of pious inattention. But the significant thing about them is that they were not words, but living fact. What Christ meant to Paul was bigger than any possible expression. He knew that the utmost he could say would fall short of what he called "the depth of the riches and wisdom and knowledge of God!" (Rom. 11:33).

But all the same he did try to express what he believed of Christ as Savior; and that gives his letters an unmatched importance. John Knox writes:

It is often said that Paul was not a theologian but rather a preacher and evangelist. . . . Now it is undoubtedly true that Paul is much more concerned to proclaim the fact of the salvation in Christ than to formulate an adequate doctrine or explanation of it; nevertheless the fact and the doctrine are inseparably connected in his mind, and one cannot understand the meaning of the fact unless one takes the doctrine into account.[4]

It would be more accurate to speak of "doctrines" rather than of "the doctrine." Paul was one of the supreme thinkers of our human race, but he was not a systematizer. His mind was too eager, too unrestingly adventurous for that. His thought was not like a candle set in some fixed place. Rather, it was like a searchlight sweeping the unbounded sky, or like the aurora that in its changing glory witnesses to some mysterious unseen force beneath the seen horizon. If there is truth in the saying that "consistency is the hobgoblin of little minds," then one of the signs of the range and vigor of the apostle's mind can be the fact that

[4] *The Interpreter's Bible, op. cit.,* IX, 368.

he did not need always to trouble to be consistent. His thinking takes many patterns, as any study of his letters shows.

There were great concepts which were in the background; and these, like everything else with Paul, came not out of abstract speculation but out of the impact upon his mind and soul of the terrible realities of life. He saw the everlasting fact of sin: not little sinnings here and there, but what seemed to be a dark, inveterate tendency in human souls to rebel against the highest. He had known what that meant in his own experience: known it in self-will and in the presumptions of pride which can turn even what was supposed to be religion into sanctimonious cruelty. In the world around him he had seen the moral degradation to which men could descend. There was the taint of continuing evil, it seemed to him, in all who could be called the sons of Adam. Christ, then, would be the "second Adam," the beginning of a new humanity. In him would come a new life of the spirit to end the dominion of the flesh.

Christ—again—could be seen as the beloved Son, come from his Father to reclaim the lost children of this earth. He had taken upon himself the consequences of all the evil of mankind. On the cross he had been the infinite, atoning sin-bearer, and in his willingness to die he had shown that there were no limits to which the redeeming love of God would fail to go. He had shown that there is a grace of God which reaches out to those who have no merit of their own. He had been like some incredible friend who comes into a court where a guilty man has been sentenced to his doom, takes that doomed man's place, and goes in his stead to ignominy and to death. He had brought the redemption that man's unworthiness could never win. And he, in his resurrection, had made men able to be lifted with him at last to victory over sin and death.

Greatly significant of Paul's thought is the benediction with which he closes his second letter to the Corinthians, the benediction which is used now in the worship of the churches everywhere. In it there is the threefold affirmation which would appear later in the Apostles' Creed and in the development of systematic doctrine, but note the words that stand first: "the grace of the Lord Jesus Christ." The ineffable new life which the disciples had seen in Jesus and which had brought to them the nearness of God—*that* was the foundation of Christian faith. This quality in Jesus which the twelve had known in their contacts with him and which Paul in his conversion had apprehended was the focus now from which all divine truth fell into perspective. Because of Jesus, in the outreach of his understanding and his mercy for the lowest and the least and his redeeming devotion that went all the way to the Cross, they could invincibly trust "the love of God." And the new power and the lift for their own living which had come into their souls, "the fellowship of the Holy Spirit," was the heavenly gift to them of the aspiration and inspired effort that would mark those for whom Jesus was the living Lord.

These—and more—were the patterns of thought in which Paul tried to express the reality that had come to him in Christ. He knew that nothing he could say would be sufficient; but the failure of words did not matter. All the while the real sufficiency existed in what Christ had done, and would do.

It can be seen that the thought of the apostle had come part of the way, but not yet all the way, toward the trinitarian creed which the Church would presently formulate. To Paul, Jesus was "the image of the invisible God, the first-born of all creation" (Col. 1:15). In Christ Jesus the living purpose of God had become incarnate, and in his crucifixion the love of God himself had made the atoning sacrifice which men in their sinfulness could never offer. Although the ministry of Christ was so completely an expression of the purpose of the Father, Paul never quite went to the point of seeing him as an equal Person in the Godhead. Jesus had come to proclaim his Father's kingdom and to bring every contrary power into subjection; but at the end, when his mission should be accomplished, the Son who had come from heaven and went back to heaven should "also be subjected to him who put all things under him," and God be recognized supreme.

This fact that not all the aspects of the ultimate creeds can be found in the words of Paul does not diminish his importance as the greatest of all first-century interpreters of Christian truth. He has not been rightly represented, but unintentionally misrepresented, by the pious theological scribes who have supposed it to be their duty to treat his thought as being both infallible and final. When that mistake has been made, it leads on to the same mistake—as we shall see—in the case of all the creeds: the mistake of supposing that form of expression must be the fixed authority, instead of remembering that the real authority is always in the living experience that must be lived again. It was this experience, not propositions, that Paul wanted to convey to all whom he could touch. The why and how of it might go beyond all definition, but in his own transformed life Paul knew that "God was in Christ reconciling the world to himself" (II Cor. 5:19), and that for every man there can be "Christ in you, the hope of glory" (Col. 1:27).

V

JOHN'S
WITNESS TO THE INCARNATE WORD

To READ ON THROUGH THE NEW TESTAMENT LOOKING FOR THE word Trinity is still to fail to find it. For it is not there. But there are increasing evidences of the kind of thinking which points in that direction.

The Fourth Gospel goes further than the letters of Paul in conceptions out of which the full doctrine of the Trinity was ultimately to emerge. The early tradition was that this Gospel had been written in his old age by John the son of Zebedee, one of the first four disciples who followed Jesus from the fishing boats by the Lake of Galilee. That view is still maintained by some scholars of learning and respected judgment, and Robert Browning, in *A Death in the Desert*, has drawn his moving imaginative picture of that beloved disciple rallying his last energy to speak to the little group of men who loved him and had brought him for shelter to a cave in the time of persecution— speaking to them as the only one now left who

> Saw with his eyes and handled with his hands
> That which was from the first, the Word of Life.

But the weight of evidence seems to be that the Gospel was not written by one of the twelve, but by someone of the next

generation, perhaps "the Elder John," of Ephesus to whom
there is a reference in the writings of Papias, Bishop of Hierapolis in the early years of the second century. Although there
are indications in the excitingly discovered Dead Sea Scrolls that
some of the forms of thought found in the Fourth Gospel may
have been familiar at a time earlier than most scholars have supposed, nevertheless it appears that the Gospel as it has come down
to us must date from as late as the end of the first century. In
nearly all, if not all, of its narrative it seems to stand at a longer
distance from the earthly life of Jesus than do Matthew, Mark,
and Luke. There is none of the vehement echo of the events
of the mid-century which comes through the letters of Paul.
For the most part, the aim of the Fourth Gospel seems to have
been not so much to recount in objective outline the events
of Jesus' ministry, but rather to perceive and to express the
eternal significance of what he did and what he was. The whole
picture is seen now in a vast perspective. What did the life and
death, the incarnation, the crucifixion, and the resurrection of
Jesus *mean* to the insights of spiritual devotion when the reality
was seen in its ultimate profundity? That was what the Gospel
of John was written to ask and to try to answer.

Archbishop William Temple wrote:

For the Word of God does not consist of printed propositions, it
is living; it is personal; it is Jesus Christ . . . The point of vital importance is the utterance of the Divine Word to the soul, the self-
communication of the Father to His children.[1]

---

[1] *Readings in St. John's Gospel.* (London: Macmillan and Co., Ltd.,
1949), ix.

That communication comes through the Incarnate Lord. In the Fourth Gospel, more expressly even that in the letters of Paul, Jesus is seen as the embodiment of the fullness of God. This is what he had become to John's own soul, and this is what John believed that from the first he must have been to those who had eyes to see and ears to hear. Therefore, it was not enough merely to repeat the particular words of Jesus which were all that verbal memory could hand down. The deeper need was to understand what the words of Jesus and the works of Jesus were really saying to those who were sensitive to understand. Accordingly in his Gospel John is not actually transmitting the sounds that fell from Jesus' lips—not even in those long chapters when he is describing Jesus as speaking to the crowd that flocked around him, to Pharisees and priests, to the disciples in the Upper Room. What the evangelist was doing seemed to him not less but more the truth than a verbatim record would have been. He was expressing the depth and wonder of what Jesus had inwardly said to him, and what he believed that Jesus, with his divine authority no longer hidden, had said and would always say to those who should be hushed to listen.

Thus, to John, the truth that came through Jesus was not limited to the words that had fallen from Jesus' lips as he walked the earth with his first disciples. John will express not only "what he remembers as having been said by Jesus in Galilee or Judaea but what he has heard the living Christ (identical and continuous with this remembered one) say in Ephesus or Alexandria." [2] To this evangelist, Jesus was more than a memory; he was an immediate reality, risen and alive.

[2] John Knox, *On the Meaning of Christ* (New York: Charles Scribner's Sons, 1947), p. 71.

And in the light of that experience which illuminated not only the present but the past, this was John's conviction: that the infinite significance of Jesus as it had come home to his own soul must have been expressing itself in Jesus' days on earth to all who had ears to hear, and in the words of his Gospel he must make that deep truth plain.

> What first were guessed as points, I now knew stars,
> And named them in the Gospel I have writ.[3]

So in the Fourth Gospel the Jesus of this evangelist's devotion could declare to his disciples, "I and the Father are one" (John 10:30), and could proclaim to those who challenged his authority, "Before Abraham was, I am" (John 8:58). In the Upper Room, on that last night before he went out to Gethsemane and the next morning to the cross, he could say: "Father, the hour has come; glorify thy Son that the Son may glorify thee, since thou hast given him power over all flesh, to give eternal life to all whom thou hast given him. And this is eternal life, that they may know thee the only true God, and Jesus Christ whom thou hast sent" (John 17:1-4).

Jesus, as John beheld him, was not only "descended from David according to the flesh, and designated Son of God in power according to the Spirit of holiness by his resurrection from the dead," as Paul had written in his letter to the Romans (1:3-4). Long before his death and resurrection, yes, from the very beginning of his ministry, Jesus knew that "the Father had given all things into his hands, and that he had come from God and was going to God" (John 13:3). When the woman of Samaria said, "I know that Messiah is coming (he who is called

[3] Browning, op. cit.

Christ); when he comes, he will show us all things," Jesus answered, "I who speak to you am he" (John 4:25-26). He could promise her, there by Jacob's well, "Whoever drinks of the water that I shall give him will never thirst; the water that I shall give him will become in him a spring of water welling up to eternal life (John 4:14). He would be "the bread of life" (6:35), "the light of the world" (8:1), "the way, and the truth, and the life" (14:6).

It is not on one level only, but on two, that this Fourth Gospel must be read. Earlier in this century there was staged an unforgettable drama called *The Eternal Road*. In the foreground of the great stage were enacted the experiences and emotions of a Jewish synagogue under persecution; but back of that immediate scene and above it were the mystical suggestions of the majestic history of the Covenant people which made the transient human movements part of the eternal road.

In the Gospel of John, similarly, there are the foreground and the background. We can comprehend the profundity of the Gospel only when we remember that there are both. The foreground is part, and only a part, of the mightier picture; but it is always there. As we have seen, John was not concerned with a detailed recital of all the objective events of Jesus' ministry; but the great central event did stand out for him with unquestionable certainty. God's revelation had been given in a human life here on this actual earth. By the time the Gospel was written there were trends of thought that treated Jesus' humanity as hardly more than an illusion. Gnosticism, moving in the thin air of philosophical speculation, with its chilled conception of a God who could be himself only as he remained remote, pictured Jesus as not much more than a *Docetic* phantom. That is to say, he only *seemed* to be a man. Knowing that representation, John would have none of it. No one of the evangelists is more emphatic about the reality of Jesus' humanness than is he. Jesus in this Fourth Gospel shares the everyday experiences of all the sons of earth. He is "wearied . . . with his journey" as he comes to Jacob's well (John 4:6). He "was deeply moved in spirit and troubled" and he "wept" at the tomb of Lazarus (John 11:33, 35). On the cross he exclaimed, "I thirst" (John 19:28). The Roman soldiers who were about to make sure that the crucifixion had done its work, "saw that he was already dead" (John 19:33). His body was carried to its tomb, "bound in linen cloths with the spices, as is the burial custom of the Jews" (John 19:40). In all things he was made flesh of our flesh.

Such is the concrete fact that is in the foreground. Then over and above it the Fourth Evangelist unfolds what are to him the infinite realities. Foreground and background merge in one perspective, so that the events of earth are seen no longer in their objectivity but in the transfiguring light of the heavenly background which, for the evangelist, was continually breaking through. For a perception of Jesus in the focus of more nearly historical recital we turn to the first three Gospels rather than to the fourth. The words recorded and some of the scenes described in the Gospel of John were not what men and women would have seen and heard with their actual eyes and ears as they gathered round the man of Nazareth. But the evangelist's conception had a vaster scope. What he recorded represented, in his belief, the truth as it was seen from the ultimate heights of the heavenly understanding.

In the Synoptic Gospels and in the writings of Paul, the interpretations of Jesus, however exalted they may be, come almost always from within the field of Hebraic thought. Jesus is Messiah, and hope for the Messiah, and the conception of him, run like a golden thread through all the climactic books of the Old Testament. Jesus is the Son; and already in the centuries when the psalms were written there was the thought of some great figure on earth adopted into special relationship to God. God's anointed servant might be able to say:

> I will tell of the decree of the Lord:
> He said to me, "You are my son,
> today I have begotten you."
>
> —Ps. 2:7

Jesus was the Son of man. The significance of that title comes from the flaming symbolism of the book of Daniel. In the Synoptic Gospels and in the letters of Paul, all this Hebrew heritage of thought and language was drawn upon in the effort to express the limitless meaning of Jesus. Now in the Fourth Gospel there are influences from another field. Jewish life and thought in the first century went on within a Greco-Roman world. Paul made a passing reference to Greek conceptions when on the Areopagus in Athens he spoke of God as "not far from each one of us, for 'in him we live and move and have our being; as even some of your poets have said'" (Acts 17:27-28). But with Paul this reference was an incidental utterance, a thing spoken, as it were, in passing. The Fourth Gospel, on the other hand, reaches out more directly to the thought forms of the surrounding culture. It will seek to use, for its interpretation of Jesus, terms adapted to wake response not only among the Jews but also among the Gentiles, not only in the Hebrew mind but also in the Greek.

So the Gospel begins with a prologue which gives a motif for all that follows. "In the beginning was the Word." "The Word" of God was a term not unfamiliar, it is true, to those who knew only the Old Testament. God's Word had been spoken of by psalmists and prophets as the expression of his purpose, the instrument for the achievement of his will. But Philo, the Jewish philosopher in Alexandria, had developed that term in a more special relationship to Hellenistic ideas. The *Word* was the Greek *Logos,* the rational principle of the Stoics which was held to give unity and moral meaning to the universe. Now the Fourth Evangelist took that term as the medium for a greater message. The Logos that would make life intelligible, the Word of God that was meant to be heard in and through his creation from the beginning, was no general principle. It was that which men had seen in Jesus. "The Word became flesh and dwelt among us." (John 1:14.) "He was in the beginning with God; all things were made through him, and without him was not anything made that was made. In him was life, and the life was the light of men." (John 1:2-4.)

When all this has been spoken and heard, it is evident that Jesus has been lifted to a height of worship which opens the gates of illimitable wonder concerning him. As this Gospel proclaims at its climax: "These are written that you may believe that Jesus is the Christ, the Son of God, and that believing you may have life in his name" (John 20:31). John's Gospel, as we have already recognized, may be of limited value as specific history. It is a retrospect rather than an immediate recital. Although we may not see the figure of Jesus as vividly as in some chapters of the Synoptics, nevertheless, it is always the Man of Nazareth who is the center of John's thought. It was Jesus, and no one but Jesus, of whom it could be believed that he "was the Word, and the Word was with God, and the Word was God" (John 1:1).

How could this be? Men's intellects were bound to ask this

question. The meaning of the eternal God made incarnate—was this something that could actually be believed? If not, then the Gospel of John was only pious imagination. But if so, then thought could not stop with the Gospel. It had to go on to those meditations concerning the nature of God and man which would result in creeds and doctrines, including the doctrine of the Trinity—meditations which might be, not the less, but the more true even though they should pass beyond the bounds of what the uninspired can conceive.

VI

THE HOLY SPIRIT

IN THE DEVELOPED DOCTRINE OF THE TRINITY THERE ARE, OF course, three elements: God the Father, God the Son, and God the Holy Spirit. We have already thought of Jesus, who would come to be regarded as the second Person in the Godhead. Now we turn to consider the basis in Scripture for belief in the Spirit as the third Person in the oneness of the triune God.

It was, of course, only at the end of a long process that such a belief could come to full expression. There have been times when biblical scholars, moved more by the piety of a priori ideas than by scrutiny of the objective facts, have read back the later concepts of the Spirit into the Old Testament. A curious instance of this may be found in the introductory note to the list of references to the Spirit in Alexander Cruden's *A Complete Concordance to the Old and New Testament*. This book is still published and familiarly used, although it was first compiled in 1737. Here is the beginning of the definition given there:

Spirit. *In* Hebrew, Ruach tr.; in Greek [πνεῦμα] pneuma. *In Scripture the word Spirit is taken,* [1] *For the Holy Ghost, the third person of the holy Trinity . . . that enlivening* Spirit *who proceeds from the Father and Son.*

But to say that is to foreshorten a long perspective. Certainly

52

the Spirit did not have such developed meaning as that for the actual consciousness of men who lived in Old Testament times. It was not part of any conceived Trinity such as would appear in the times to come. What the Spirit did mean in Old Testament thought must be looked for within the framework of what men did actually think concerning God.

To the Hebrew people the Almighty God was supremely a God of action. He was never indifferent or passive. The events of history were not accidents, nor did they come from any devisings of men. It was God's hand that controlled them. It was God also of whom all living things on earth could say, "thou openest thine hand, they are filled with good" (Ps. 104:28 K.J.V.). But always in the Hebrew mind there was a fearsome sense of God's awful majesty. His very name of Yahweh was too sacred to be spoken aloud. No one could look upon his face and live. When men in Israel told of God's coming down to touch their lives, they might tell of him as coming through an angel whom he had sent, or they might speak of his coming through his Spirit.

In the pages of the Old Testament, the Spirit appears first as God's creative power. When "the earth was without form and void, and darkness was upon the face of the deep," then "the Spirit of God was moving over the face of the waters." So begins the book of Genesis (Gen. 1:2). At the climax of the 104th psalm, with its long panorama of the wonders of the sky and the earth and the sea, comes a similar reference: "When thou sendeth forth thy Spirit, they are created" (Ps. 104:30). This creative Spirit might be thought of as the breath of God. "The Lord God formed man of the dust of the ground, and breathed into his nostrils the breath of life; and man became a living soul." (Gen. 2:7 K.J.V.) So also "the Spirit of the Lord" came to the prophet Ezekiel in the valley where he saw his vision of dry bones and proclaimed, "Behold, I will cause breath to enter you, and you shall live" (Ezek. 37:5).

Sometimes the Spirit was the energy that came to a man to enlarge his powers for special work appointed him to do, as when Moses chose Bezalel to build the tabernacle because the Lord had "filled him with the Spirit of God, with ability, with intelligence, with knowledge, and with all craftsmanship" (Exod. 35:31). And it was written in the book of Judges that when God was ready to bring deliverance to Israel from the Midianite invaders, "the Spirit of the Lord took possession of Gideon" (6:34) and made him into the "mighty man of valor" that he became (6:12).

Often in the Old Testament the Spirit came in religious ecstasy. So "the Lord came down in the cloud and spoke to [Moses], and took some of the spirit that was upon him and put it upon the seventy elders; and when the spirit rested upon them, they prophesied" (Num. 11:25). Similarly, when Saul encountered the band of frenzied devotees at Gibeathelohim, it came to pass as Samuel had told him, that "the spirit of the Lord will come mightily upon you, and you shall prophesy with them and be turned into another man" (I Sam. 10:6).

But in the latter part of the Old Testament the Spirit has a loftier meaning. It represents the moving of God, not only in creation, or in the breathing into man of physical life, or in religious ecstasy; but in the awakening of men's minds and souls to God's highest purposes for them. Prophecy becomes not uncontrolled excitement, but an exaltation to new levels of awareness of the will of God. "Not by might, nor by power, but by my Spirit, says the Lord of hosts" was the way the word of God came to his servant according to the prophet Zechariah

(4:6). "I will put my spirit within you, and cause you to walk in my statutes and be careful to obscure my ordinances" was the promise that Ezekiel heard (Ezek. 36:27). And Deutero-Isaiah, when he sought to tell how God had commissioned him, expressed it thus:

> The Spirit of the Lord God is upon me,
>   because the Lord has anointed me
> to bring good tidings to the afflicted;
>   he has sent me to bind up the brokenhearted,
> to proclaim liberty to the captives,
>   and the opening of the prison to those who are
>   bound.
>
> —Isa. 61:1

It was with the declaration that those words of the prophet had been fulfilled that Jesus startled the men and women of Nazareth on the Sabbath day when, for the first time, he stood up to speak in the synagogue of his home town. Yet in the over-all record of the Synoptic Gospels explicit references to the Spirit are not so numerous as one might suppose they would be.

In the Gospel of Mark there are six, five of which are paralleled in Matthew and Luke, and the remaining one paralleled in Matthew. John the Baptist, who was baptizing with water, declared that Jesus "will baptize you with the Holy Spirit" (Mark 1:8, Matt. 3:11; Luke 3:16). When Jesus himself was baptized, "he saw the heavens opened and the Spirit descending upon him like a dove" (Mark 1:10; Matt. 3:16; Luke 3:22). After the baptism, it was the Spirit that immediately drove him out into the wilderness" (Mark 1:12; Matt. 4:1; Luke 4:1). Preaching to the people in Galilee, Jesus said: "Truly, I say to you, all sins will be forgiven the sons of men, and whatever blasphemies they utter; but whosoever blasphemes against the Holy Spirit never has forgiveness, but is guilty of an eternal sin" (Mark 3:28-29; Matt. 12:31-32; Luke 12:10). In the temple in Jerusalem Jesus spoke of David as "inspired by the Holy Spirit" (Mark 12:36; Matt. 22:43). And to the disciples, as he foresaw the peril and the persecution that might be drawing near for them, he said: "Do not be anxious beforehand what you are to say; but say whatever is given you in that hour, for it is not you who speak, but the Holy Spirit" (Mark 13:11; Matt. 10:19-20; Luke 12:11-12).

In the Gospel of Matthew there are five references to the Spirit which occur in that Gospel alone. The Virgin "is found to be with child of the Holy Spirit" (1:18); and as Joseph considered this, an angel of the Lord, appearing in a dream, tells him not to be dismayed, "for that which is conceived in her is of the Holy Spirit" (1:20). The preaching of Jesus was said to be a fulfillment of the prophecy of Isaiah, "I will put my Spirit upon him, and he shall proclaim justice to the Gentiles" (12:18). To the Pharisees, who refused to recognize the meaning of his ministry, Jesus says, "If it is by the Spirit of God that I cast out demons, then the kingdom of God has come upon you" (12:28). After the resurrection, according to Matthew, Jesus gave to his disciples in Galilee the final charge, "Go therefore and make disciples of all nations, baptizing them in the name of the Father and of the Son and of the Holy Spirit" (28:19).

Seven more references to the Spirit occur in Luke. As Matthew had told of the angelic messages to Joseph, so Luke tells that an angel said to Mary, "The Holy Spirit will come upon you, and the power of the Most High will overshadow you" (1:34). So also it was promised for the birth of John the Baptist that "he will be filled with the Holy Spirit" (1:15) Elizabeth, John's mother-to-be was "filled with the Holy Spirit" when she greeted Mary (1:41) and so was Zechariah as he lifted up his thanksgiving after John was born (1:67). It was "in the power of the Spirit" that Jesus returned into Galilee on the Sabbath when he preached in Nazareth (4:14). Jesus "rejoiced in the Holy Spirit" when (as Matthew also records) there came to him the ineffable consciousness that "All things have been delivered to me by my Father; and no one knows who the Son is except the Father, or who the Father is except the Son" (10:22; Matt. 11:27). And finally Luke gives this as a saying of Jesus: "If you then, who are evil, know how to give good gifts to your children, how much more will the heavenly Father give the Holy Spirit to those who ask him?" (11:13).

So the Holy Spirit as reflected in the Synoptic Gospels follows the likeness seen in the latter part of the Old Testament. The Spirit comes as God's creative and illuminating power. It is also God's redeeming goodness—goodness so evident that it is possible to deny it only by a deliberate perversion of conscience which makes a man willfully deaf and blind. Blasphemy against the Spirit, therefore, is not any ordinary and unwitting sin; and those sensitive persons, always to be found, who grow pitifully afraid that they may somehow have been guilty of the sin against the Spirit are the ones most unlikely ever to have committed it. The ultimate sin belongs only to those who incorrigibly treat goodness as something to be despised and make evil into their good. All the while, according to the words of Jesus in the Lucan passage already quoted, if even sinful human beings give good gifts to their children, "much more will the heavenly Father give the Holy Spirit to those who ask him."

In the book of Acts, with its story of the early Church, recorded experience of the Holy Spirit runs through the chapters like a spreading flame. Fifty-two times in Acts some vital occurrence is attributed directly to the Spirit—the Holy Spirit that counsels, guides, empowers.

In the upper room in Jerusalem, the Spirit came to the disciples like a mighty wind and like tongues of fire. It was with a promise of the gift of the Spirit that Peter ended his sermon on Pentecost; and it was because he was "filled with the Holy Spirit" that he dared proclaim Christ before the high priests who had arrested him.

It was the Holy Spirit that glorified the face of the martyr Stephen; the Holy Spirit that guided Philip to interpret the gospel to the Ethiopian officer; the Holy Spirit that commanded Peter to answer the message from Cornelius, the centurion. It was the Holy Spirit that was given to Paul at his conversion, and that was to be the immediate directing influence in great moments of his life which the book of Acts goes on to record. It was for the gift of the Holy Spirit that the apostles prayed when they laid their hands on the new converts in Samaria who had "received the word of God"; and it was the Holy Spirit that completed what had been lacking for the disciples of John the Baptist whom Paul found at Ephesus, when they were "baptized in the name of the Lord Jesus."

No one who reads the book of Acts can fail to recognize there the Holy Spirit as a transfiguring power. For those who followed "the Way" of Jesus, "the Holy Spirit was a present and living experience. This was God alive among them and within them. And by his Spirit everything else came alive—the Scriptures, the Church, themselves." [1]

[1] David H. C. Read, *The Christian Faith* (New York: Charles Scribner's Sons, 1956), p. 94.

At the same time it is a fact that human conception of what should be sought from God is not always on the highest level. In every generation there may appear and reappear the inveterate tendency to want the kind of gifts from God that will fit into the framework of natural desires. It can be so with the gift of the Spirit. In religious experiences of the Old Testament at their more primitive level, as with the band of so-called prophets whom the young Saul encountered, possession by the Spirit could find its expression in physical excitement—with wild music and dancing and the emotional frenzy that seemed to the devotees to lift them out of their ordinary selves into a supernatural ecstasy.

In the early Christian Church, simple folk with their immature conceptions could reach out for that sort of satisfaction and suppose it to be the real religion. The apostle Paul encountered that in Corinth. The fourteenth chapter of his first letter to the Corinthians shows the ecstatic fervor which he had to deal with —and to try to turn into a deeper understanding. He himself knew that there can be a kind of ecstasy which can be like an ineffable tide flooding in to fill the shallowness of a human soul, or like the wings of angels lifting the spirit up to God. "I know a man in Christ," he wrote in his second letter to the Corinthians (II Cor. 12:2-4), "who fourteen years ago was caught up to the third heaven—whether in the body or out of the body I do not know, God knows. And I know that this man was caught up into Paradise . . . and he heard things that cannot be told, which man may not utter." But Paul knew that the ultimate manifestation of the Spirit was not in emotional rapture; it was in the mind illumined and in the will inspired for the service of God in Christ.

In this sense references to the Spirit ring like recurring music through all the letters of Paul. "Be aglow with the Spirit," he wrote to the church in Rome; "serve the Lord" (Rom. 12:11). "The kingdom of God does not mean food and drink but right-eousness and peace and joy in the Holy Spirit." (Rom. 14:17.) He reminded the little company of Christians in Thessalonica that though the gospel came to them "in much affliction" it came to them also "with joy inspired by the Holy Spirit," and "in power" and "with full conviction" (I Thess. 1:6, 5). So they should "not quench the Spirit," that the God of peace might sanctify them wholly (I Thess. 5:19, 23).

"God's love has been poured into our hearts through the Holy Spirit which has been given to us," the apostle wrote (Rom. 5:5). From the Spirit there would come a new dimension of life: release from old inhibitions, moral strengthening, and a lift of the soul due, not to its own resources, but to a grace given it from above. "The law of the Spirit of life in Christ Jesus has set me free from the law of sin and death." (Rom. 8:2.) "Those who live according to the Spirit set their minds on the things of the Spirit. To set the mind on the flesh is death, but to set the mind on the Spirit is life and peace." (Rom. 8:5, 6.) By "the power of the Holy Spirit" even the humble Christian could "abound in hope" (Rom. 15:13) and believe that the fruit of the Spirit would be "love, joy, peace, patience, kindness, goodness, faithfulness, gentleness, self-control" (Gal. 5:22).

Thus for Paul the Spirit was a living influence of immense significance; the fact of that is unmistakable. It is when we come to the question of exactly how Paul conceived the origin and nature of the Spirit that the answer is not so clear. Cyril C. Richardson in *The Doctrine of the Trinity* [2] has indicated the uncertainty that comes to the inquirer who tries to analyze Paul's

[2] (Nashville: Abingdon Press, 1958.)

words and summarize his thought. "The Spirit in Paul is distinguished both from the Father and from Christ. On that question there can be no doubt." [3] But how is the Spirit related to the Father? On the one hand there is the suggestion given in I Cor. 2:10-11 where Paul is speaking of the "hidden wisdom" of God's redeeming purpose which now "God has revealed to us through the Spirit." Then he continues,

For the Spirit searches everything, even the depths of God. For what person knows a man's thought except the spirit of the man which is in him? So also no one comprehends the thoughts of God except the Spirit of God.

From these words there comes the impression that Paul is thinking of the Spirit as something more intimate than God's creative energy sent out as his instrument.

It is not merely God's breath, but his self-awareness, his mind, his inner being. This may be the source or seat of God's vitality, but it is more. It is his self-consciousness, his very being, the center of his "person," as we might say. Just as a man's spirit is his ultimate reality, when he is stripped of all that is accidental to his being, so God's Spirit is his inner self. Spirit therefore contrasts with Christ, insofar as the latter is God's image, while the former is his inner being.[4]

That is one aspect of the Spirit in Paul's conception. But as Richardson points out:

Paul does not stop there. He introduces yet another theme which is really incongruous with this. In Rom. 8:26 ff., he deals with the Spirit as if he were an entity distinct from the Father, standing over

[3] *Ibid.,* p. 49.
[4] *Ibid.,* p. 50.

against him and having a mind of his own. The Spirit, says Paul, intercedes for us in prayer; and God, who searches men's hearts, knows what is the "mind" of the Spirit, because the Spirit intercedes in accordance with God's will. Thus the Spirit here, far from being God's inner self, is distinguished from this. He is a heavenly "power" of God—over against the Father—with a mind of his own and operating in the Christian heart.

There is no way to draw together these diverse themes in Paul. In one the Spirit is identical with God's being, in the other he stands over against it. The fact is that Paul has put forward ideas which do not fully harmonize. What, however, may be said further is this: In one sense the Spirit, as God's inner being, is identical with the Father and as such clearly distinguishable from Christ. In the other sense the Spirit is a heavenly power whereby we are aided in our prayers and feel God himself is praying within us. This comes very close to being the same thing as the indwelling Christ.[5]

So Paul's thought can never be tied up in one neat and systematic package. Theological scholars with their passion for finality of statement have always tried to do that, but inevitably they have failed. Paul himself was too much a man possessed by the Spirit to be held down to meticulous ratiocination. His supreme concern was not so much to explain as to convey the living reality of his experience; not so much to shape ideas as to implant conviction. Of course his mind did blaze into great ideas as he tried to express the meaning of what he inwardly felt and knew. It was inevitable—and also right—that these ideas should be seized upon by the devoted men who afterwards would try to build the structure of what could be proper theological beliefs. What Paul had said about Christ and about the Holy Spirit would have immense influence in the shaping of creeds and of

[5] *Ibid.*, pp. 50-51.

doctrines such as that of the doctrine of the Trinity, in regard to which—as we shall consider presently—there may be two conclusions. One will be the recognition that whenever we are seized in the doctrines by the vital reality of the religious experience that was in Paul, then we have come into contact with the living truth. The other is the knowledge that we have a right to freedom of the mind: the reverent freedom that will analyze doctrinal formulations to see whether or not, and to what degree, their forms succeed in expressing the spiritual facts which must be made repeatable in life.

Whatever may ultimately be said about the rich complexity of Paul's thought, *this* is certain: If the Spirit had vast significance for him, it was because the Spirit somehow brought to him that which was for him precious above everything—namely, a realized communion with the living Christ. The relative values in the mind cannot be measured by arithmetic; but, all the same, there is arresting suggestion in the letters of Paul for any reader who begins to note Paul's references to the Spirit and his references to Christ. There is no doubt as to which was the great undergirding influence on which other conceptions were lifted up and carried like ships on a flood tide. The risen Lord is spoken of with many names: Jesus, Jesus our Lord, Jesus Christ, Christ Jesus, our Lord Jesus Christ, Lord Jesus, the Son. But all of them alike mean the one Master by whom Paul's life, since the vision on the Damascus road, had been possessed. In the first letter to the Thessalonians, Paul speaks of the Spirit four times and of Jesus, his Lord and Christ, under one of his many names or titles, twenty-five times. In the letter to the Galatians, of the Spirit sixteen times and of Christ forty-two times; in the letter to the Romans, of the Spirit twenty-eight times and of Christ ninety; in first Corinthians, of the Spirit twenty-three times and of Christ one-hundred-five. When one comes to the last letters, in which Paul may have been instinctively expressing what had been his dominant reliance through all his life, one will find that in Philippians, where the Spirit appears twice, Christ is spoken of forty-seven times; and in Colossians, where the Spirit only once is named, twenty-nine times there comes the name of Christ.

As we have already noted, it is not possible to know specifically what may have been Paul's conception of the relation of the Spirit to God the Father, or to tell how far his thought may have been moving toward what would later appear as the trinitarian doctrine of the Holy Spirit as a third Person in the Godhead. However that may have been, *this* sure fact shines through: that for Paul the one perfect work of the Spirit was to make men's minds and hearts sensitive to the saving meaning of Jesus who had lived, been crucified, and risen from the dead, and to bring this living Jesus home to them as the indwelling Christ. "Because you are sons, God has sent the Spirit of his Son into our hearts," Paul wrote to the Galatians (4:6). The great longing that he had for all Christian souls broke into expression in his cry, "My little children, with whom I am again in travail until Christ be formed in you!" (4:19).

This matter of what the criterion for recognition of the Spirit ought to be comes close to religious actualities. There are contemporary sects which promise special manifestations of the Spirit and which have a degree of fervor that some Christians might wish they also had. But the danger is that there can be invocations of the Spirit—the chief result of which is emotional excitement, so that men and women "speak with tongues" or become ecstatic "Holy Rollers"—without remembering that the decisive test of Christianity is not in excited feeling, but in steady effort to make the facts of everyday behavior square with the Spirit which those who looked at Jesus saw in him.

In the Fourth Gospel the Spirit, under one or another name, is referred to oftener than in any one of the Synoptics; but the thought in the evangelist's mind is more complex and more elusive.

Attention is arrested first by the prologue. Here the creative energy of God is expressed not as the Spirit, but as the *Logos*, the *Word* of God. It is true, on the one hand, that the Word is an authentic echo from the Old Testament. As the Hebrew *dabar*, and in the Greek translation of the Septuagint as the *Logos*, the Word appears as the expression of God's uttered message to the prophets and as the effective power of his will. Isaiah, for example, saw the word of the Lord, and prophesied that "out of Zion shall go forth the law, and the word of the Lord from Jerusalem" (2:3).

It is also true that the prologue reflects an influence that comes from another direction. The evangelist is seeking to represent the eternal significance of Christ in terms that will reach not only the Hebrew but also the Hellenistic mind. Philo of Alexandria—as has been noted—had made the thought of the creative Logos a conception currently familiar; therefore, when the evangelist wanted his conviction of the timelessness of Christ to be understood in all the Greco-Roman world, he wrote as he did. After this language that serves his special purpose in the prologue, he begins presently to speak specifically of the Spirit; and at first his thought of the nature and the role of the Spirit seem to be equated with that of the Synoptics. But at the climax of his Gospel—as we shall see—there appears a difference.

In the account of Jesus' baptism the Spirit appears in essentially the same way as in Mark, Matthew, and Luke—descending upon Jesus as a dove from heaven (1:32). In the third chapter, with its description of the visit of Nicodemus, the Spirit is more mystical. Jesus speaks of "that which is born of the Spirit"; and "he whom God has sent utters the words of God, for it is not by measure that he gives the Spirit" (3:5, 34). In the next chapter, which tells of Jesus' conversation with the woman of Samaria, it is difficult to know whether the evangelist means, in the words he puts upon the lips of Jesus, to speak of the Spirit as an entity in God, or instead, as the generalized reality of that which is spiritual and heavenly as distinguished from the material and the earthly. "The true worshipers will worship the Father in spirit and truth" (4:23): with insignificant differences such as between "shall" and "will," that is what we read in both the King James and the Revised Standard translations of the Gospel. But where the King James translators represent Jesus as saying "God is a Spirit," with the capital letter, the later scholars, at the end of long pondering of the text and context of the manuscripts, write instead "God is spirit"—who is to be worshiped "in spirit and truth" (4:24).

The next time the Spirit is mentioned, there is a new and different significance in the thought that it conveys. Speaking in Jerusalem "on the last day of the feast" [of Tabernacles], Jesus spoke about the Spirit, "which those who believed in him were to receive; for as yet the Spirit had not been given, because Jesus was not yet glorified" (7:37, 39). On the last night, in the Upper Room, Jesus said to the disciples, "I will pray the Father, and he will give you another Counselor, to be with you for ever, even the Spirit of truth"; and again: "The Counselor, the Holy Spirit, whom the Father will send in my name, he will teach you all things, and bring to your remembrance all that I have said to you" (14:16, 26). Also on that same night he told the disciples what then they could not comprehend: that it would be to their advantage that he should leave them, since only after his going would "the Counselor" come to them, "the Spirit of truth ... who will take what is mine and declare it to you" (16:7, 14). Then, after the resurrection, Jesus appeared again to the disciples in Jerusalem, "breathed on them, and said to them, 'Receive the Holy Spirit'" (20:22).

Here, manifestly, there has come a new dimension to the biblical representation of the Spirit. He is more now than that creative aspect of God which the Old Testament knew. He could not have been fully comprehended until men had first seen the meaning of God in Jesus. Now the Holy Spirit would carry to men's inner awareness the companionship of the invisible but everliving Christ. So the Gospels move a step further toward what was to become a developed doctrine of the Trinity, and toward the Nicene Creed's declaration of belief "in the Holy Ghost ... who proceedeth from the Father *and* the Son."

VII

ATTEMPTED
EXPLANATIONS OF THE FAITH

IT WILL BE SEEN THAT THE *roots* OF WHAT WOULD GROW INTO
the doctrine of the Trinity were present from the beginning in
what Christian disciples—not only seers and saints, but also the
simple people—felt and inwardly knew. They were inheritors
of the profound faith of Israel in one God, the Almighty, who
held all creation in his hands. They had learned in a new way
the grace of God that came to them when they thought of Jesus
and tried to follow him. And they were sure that there was something stirring in their souls, to bless them and to strengthen them,
which was not of their own making and could be nothing less
than the Spirit of God. On the ground of daily reality, all that
was plain.

But on another level, all was not so plain. How could that
which had been experienced be intellectually interpreted? To
believe that what men had experienced spiritually must be true
was one thing; to get it into an intellectual framework which
would seem consistent with the whole of truth was something
further. Yet because the human mind can never be quiescent, it
was inevitable that thinkers in the early Christian Church would
go on to something further. They would try to interpret and to
explicate—with a purpose that was right, but through processes
of reasoning which were bound to be mixed in their result.

The first question had to do with the Incarnation. What did it mean to say that God had been in Jesus, and what new concepts of God came from that belief?

Through the long history of the people of Israel there had been the immense conviction of God's existence. He was always *there*: awful and often hidden, but never to be forgotten as the power that might at any moment break in to turn their destiny this way or that. As they belonged to him, so they thought at first that he belonged to them, *their* God of benefits, of battles, even of vengeance when they needed vengeance. Later the prophets saw him as the God of all the nations, the Righteous One by whom all peoples would be judged. Then came the increasing faith that he was the God not only of general judgment, but of infinite compassion. "Like as a father pitieth his children, so the Lord pitieth them that fear him." (Ps. 103:13 K.J.V.)

Because of Jesus there was a new element for Christians in their thought of God. They felt that the reality of God had come close to them in him. It was not enough to think of him only in the Old Testament terms as the Messiah, the anointed servant of the Lord sent to accomplish a particular mission. The relationship was deeper and more ultimate than that. According to John's Gospel, Jesus himself had said, "I and the Father are one" (John 10:30). Paul in one of his letters to the Corinthians had spoken of "the glory of Christ, who is the likeness of God" (II Cor. 4:4). And in the Epistle to the Hebrews it was written that he reflected "the glory of God and bears the very stamp of his nature" (Heb. 1:3).

How then to conceive and to put into words this bond between Jesus and the infinite Father?

One familiar concept was as the Son. Jesus himself had often used that word. It sounds again and again in the letters of Paul;

69

and the first sentence of Hebrews is the declaration that God who "spoke of old to our fathers by the prophets . . . in these last days . . . has spoken to us by a Son."

It is true that the word Son had been used before without this infinite significance. Some human figure, destined for an exalted role in God's service, might be designated as God's son. So in the second psalm, which belongs to the pre-exilic period of Israel's history and was apparently written as a hymn to celebrate a king's accession, the sixth and seventh verses represent first the divine proclamation and then the response of the one who has been anointed:

> I have set my King
> On Zion, my holy hill

and then,

> I will tell of the decree of the Lord:
> He said to me, "You are my son,
>   Today I have begotten you."

Even the word "begotten" has there no metaphysical suggestion. Both in Egypt and in Babylonia a king was often thought of as the offspring of a god, but such a thought was not in the Hebrew mind. Rather, the words "You are my son, today I have begotten you" were an echo of the familiar form for an adoption of a child, which was as old as the Code of Hammurabi. For the psalmist the ethical suggestion was predominant. Some royal person was declared to be God's son because God would make him fit to be the instrument of his will.

But in the New Testament the conception of the relationship between Jesus and the Father goes beyond the Old Testament idea of one who is made God's son—although not, perhaps, at first. Peter's sermon on Pentecost seems to imply that Jesus had been "a man attested to you by God with mighty works and wonders and signs which God did through him in your midst," and that God had taken this man Jesus, and by his crucifixion and resurrection had "made him both Lord and Christ" (Acts 2:22, 36). Even Paul, in his letter to the Romans, speaks of the "Son . . . descended from David according to the flesh and designated Son of God in power according to the Spirit of holiness by his resurrection from the dead" (Rom. 1:3-4). But in the letter to the Philippians Paul's thought—or at any rate his expression of it—has a new dimension. He writes that "Christ Jesus . . . was in the form of God"; it was "equality with God" which he in himself possessed, and his life on earth was a laying aside of this equality with God, that he might empty himself, take the form of a servant, and be "born in the likeness of men" (Phil. 2:6). In the letter to the Colossians he wrote that "He is the image of the invisible God, the first-born of all creation" (Col. 1:15). And in the prologue of the Gospel of John the thought has risen to this: "We have beheld his glory, glory as of the only Son from the Father. . . . No one has ever seen God; the only Son, who is in the bosom of the Father, he has made him known" (John 1:14, 18).

The theologians of the early Christian centuries built on these foundations, which were originally Hebrew and scriptural; meanwhile they were also increasingly influenced by the Hellenistic thinking which was inescapable in their world and time.

But from the beginning there were complications. As long as Jesus was looked upon as God's servant adopted into a special relationship for the carrying out of God's will on earth, the thought-form could be simple. But if he were not only Jesus of the human ministry, not only Christ as Messiah of the Old

71

Testament concrete hope, but the Son, who before all time was one with the Father, then there was a double difficulty. On the one hand, how could this be reconciled with the awed monotheism that was the heart of Jewish orthodoxy? On the other hand, what reckoning should be made with the Greek conception of the Absolute who in his everlasting transcendence must be remote from all other than himself?

All the while, notwithstanding what surface indications might incline us to assume, the theologians of the Church were dominated by a purpose which to them was not abstract. Their profound concern was religious, not academic. The truth about them is suggested by the title of this book, the title which not only in its words but in the order of its words embodies an emphasis which must not be forgotten. *Trinity* was not the first word, but the last one; the first was *Jesus*. The great Christian thinkers, no matter how high and far their minds might go, started from that which they held as vital to their souls. What was vital was the *fact* that Jesus had become for those who followed him a living Christ whose boundless significance they were trying to express. The expression they developed had to find its way through trial and error; and the test for them as between truth *or* error was not a doctrine already formulated but the progressive charting of a course like the course of a ship, which would avoid the reefs and flats of shallowness and the rocks of contradiction and find the open channel along which an understanding of Christ could go upon its mighty way.

That being so, the positive directions in Christian thinking would be influenced by the dangers, sometimes the hidden and only partly charted dangers—that had to be avoided. The Church's faith in Christ was turned toward infinite horizons;

but, in between, the pilots of the Church's thinking had to see the errors on which it could be wrecked.

Early among these was the teaching of the so-called Ebionites. These were the Jewish Christians who had fled from Jerusalem before the siege and capture of the city by Titus in A.D. 70, had settled for a while in the region of the Dead Sea, and in the first and second centuries might still affect the Christian fellowship. They represented essentially the same inflexible insistence upon the forms of Judaism from which Paul had devoted his life to set the churches free. The more extreme Ebionites denied and rejected the apostleship of Paul altogether. They insisted that circumcision was still necessary to salvation and that all the Mosaic ceremonial ordinances were binding. The less rigid Ebionites did not reject Paul's gospel that carried Christ to the Gentiles, but they wanted, nevertheless, to hold to the Old Testament ordinances for themselves. As Jerome was afterwards to describe them, "since they wish to be both Jews and Christians, they are neither Jews nor Christians."

Here again was a threatened limitation of the universal saviorhood of Christ. Paul had countered this by his insistence that even to the Jews God's redeeming promise had not come first on condition of their obedience to the Law; it had come to Abraham on the sole ground of his faith in that undeserved promise, and could therefore come in the same way to the Gentiles. Then, in the second century, Christian thought began to draw the wider corollaries from Paul's message and also from the prologue of the Gospel of John. Christ was "the true light that enlightens every man" (John 1:9)—not only every Jew, but every man.

Had the goodness in all good men of all times and in all peoples therefore been due to some reflection in them of the same Christ

73

whom men saw manifest at last in the face of Jesus? Such was the question which men could ask themselves as they related the Christian gospel to the history, not only of Judaism, but of the world at large. They began to answer it in such terms as those of one of the earliest of the post-apostolic fathers whose writings have survived, Justin, called Justin Martyr because of his death in A.D. 162 during the persecution in the reign of Marcus Aurelius. As Alexander V. G. Allen says of him in *The Continuity of Christian Thought*:

> Justin is the first writer among the ancient Fathers to assert the truth that God had revealed Himself to the heathen world as well as to the Jewish people, that He had done so not merely through some subordinate process in external nature, but through his Son, who is the divine reason in every man.[1]

Thus for Justin the dimensions of the revelation that came in Jesus were enlarged. The Word that "became flesh and dwelt among us" (John 1:14)—and thus was first fully known in the Incarnate One—had been speaking always to the hearts of men in so far as they would listen and try to obey that which dimly, at least, they could understand.

Thus, as Justin taught, there had been a spiritual and essential Christ, not limited by conditions of time and space, of whom every race of men had been in some degree partakers. There was inspiring suggestion here. Yet in the realm of thinking which Justin offered there could be danger. It was the danger that Christ might be interpreted as a general diffused principle, and the crucial reality of an Incarnation be forgotten or denied.

That was what actually happened in the rise of Gnosticism.

[1] (Boston: Houghton Mifflin Co., 1884), p. 30.

74

As George Park Fisher has defined it in his *History of Christian Doctrine:*

> Gnosticism may be described as an eclectic philosophy in which heathen, Jewish, and Christian elements [were] commingled in various proportions, giving rise to a diversity of systems, the ideas of these systems being incorporated in mythical or mythological forms.[2]

It was in the second century that Gnosticism was most elaborately developed and aggressively taught, but already in the first century the existence of Gnostic thinking is evident as an influence which some of the New Testament writers recognize and warn against. For the fundamental aspects of Gnosticism were these: that it claimed to bring a new *gnosis* (knowledge) in contrast with the *pistis* (faith) such as Paul had preached, an esoteric knowledge available to the intellectually initiated. An element of this *gnosis* was a conception of God that linked him with the world, not directly, but by a chain of mediating powers which the initiated must understand. In this philosophy for the supposedly learned, as it was fully formulated in the second century by Saturninus in Syria, Basilides in Alexandria, Valentinus in Alexandria and Rome, there were differences in detail, but there was an over-all likeness in that the Jesus of the Gospels faded in a cloudland of theoretical speculation as to how God could be revealed. All the Gnostic schools of thought were shaped by the conception that God, by the necessity of his awful holiness, must dwell apart from any contact with things finite and created, and, therefore, that the making of the material world and the ordering of actual human history came through lower beings who descended in a long gradation from him who is the unknowable.

[2] (New York: Charles Scribner's Sons, 1896), p. 51.

For example: to follow the graphic summary of Fisher—in the Syrian formulation of Saturninus—

The highest God, the "Father Unknown," creates a realm of spirits in descending gradations, the spirits of the seven planets being on the lowest stage. By them, or by the Demiurge at their head, the visible world was made and also man. The Demiurge is the God of the Jews. . . . The good God sends an Aeon, Nous, who appears in an unreal body as a Saviour to deliver the spiritual class, not only from Satan, but also from the Demiurge and the associated planetary spirits. The means of deliverance embrace abstinence from marriage and other forms of asceticism.[3]

The ideas of Basilides and of Valentinus similarly changed the concrete message of the Gospels into a shadow-show of philosophical abstractions. "The Head of all things," according to Basilides, "is The Being who is pure nothing; i.e., nothing concrete, the Ineffable One." The kind of actual redemption which Christians knew in their own experinece faded out into esoteric theory—theory that could seem no nearer to ordinary people than spectral northern lights, flickering from below the far horizon of their own world. Jesus was no longer the real man who in his living and dying linked humanity with God. Instead, according to Valentinus, it was only a "psychical Christ" who was crucified.

More influential than the teachers already named was Marcion, born in Asia Minor, who came to Rome about A.D. 140. He had been deeply moved by the gospel as he believed that Paul had preached it, especially by the contrast between the Jewish trust in salvation by the law and salvation by God's free grace through the love of Christ. He came to the conclusion, therefore, that

[3] *Ibid.*, pp. 56-57.

the Old Testament had nothing genuinely to do with Christianity. The Jews belonged, he taught, not to the God of love, but to the inferior Demiurge, who had promised them a world-conquering Messiah who would be the instrument of judgment and of Jewish vengeance upon the other peoples of the earth. But here the God of love intervened. He descended to earth in the reign of Tiberius in an unreal body, as though he were the Messiah that the Demiurge had promised. But the Demiurge, who was the Prince and power of this earth, saw that Jesus disregarded the law which he, the Demiurge, had given to the Jews; and so he caused Jesus to be crucified. But Jesus, according to Marcion, did not really suffer, because he who had come from God was only seemingly in a human body. In what appeared to be Jesus' death, the Demiurge was defeated and his power once for all destroyed.

As one looks back upon the Gnostic teachings, they may seem to have been such fantastic theorizings that one may wonder how they could have been important. But they had the subtle fascination of what was alleged to be a superior knowledge, through which, therefore, a man might be saved by pride of intellect without the constant submission of his life to the redeeming spirit manifested in the actual Jesus. Gnosticism, with its assumption of a long gradation of powers between the high God and the actual world of men, could destroy the essential Christian faith that, once men had experienced the saving grace of God through Jesus, there were no competing realities which they needed superstitiously to fear. That was the vital meaning in some of the words of Paul—words which from our perspective may not at first stand out in their sharp significance, but did actually refer to dangers which were real then, and in different terms may be continually repeated. He wrote in his letter to the Colossians,

See to it that no one makes a prey of you by philosophy and empty deceit, according to human tradition, according to the elemental spirits of the universe, and not according to Christ. For in him dwells the whole fullness of deity bodily, and you have come to fullness of life in him, who is the head of all rule and authority.
—Col. 2:8, 9

Paul's thought, with its sense of the illimitable dimensions of the gospel, could rise into heights of infinite wonder; but like Wordsworth's *Sky-Lark*, he was a

Type of the wise who soar, but never roam;
True to the kindred points of Heaven and Home.

That which to him was "the mystery hidden for ages and generations" (Col. 1:26) had come home to earth in the man Christ Jesus; and in him, and not in some phantom of philosophy, men must find their Savior.

So also John understood, and therefore he wrote in his first letter:

Beloved, do not believe every spirit, but test the spirits to see whether they are of God; for many false prophets have gone out into the world. By this you know the Spirit of God: every spirit which confesses that Jesus Christ has come in the flesh is of God, and every spirit which does not confess Jesus is not of God.
—I John 4:1, 2

That same emphasis was continued by the men who carried on the central stream of Christian thinking. They lived in the same world as did the Gnostics, and like them they were affected by the universal influence of Greek philosophy—as would be conspicuously evident at length in the creeds of Nicaea and Chalcedon. They were trying to build an intellectual framework for the Christian faith that would be lofty enough to contain its illimitable truth. But they shunned the halfway theological fancifulness of the Gnostics, and they kept their thought of the universal Christ linked to history and to the reality of Jesus. "Our Lord Jesus Christ," wrote Irenaeus, "who did, through his transcendent love, become what we are, that He might bring us to be even what He is Himself." [4] Clement of Alexandria, maintaining both the full humanity and the full divinity of Christ, said "The Word of God became man that thou mayest learn from man how man may become God." [5] In the creed in use at Rome by the middle of the first century, embodying the substance of what in its full development was to be called "the Apostles' Creed," the Christ who was proclaimed as sitting "at the right hand of the Father" was the Jesus who had lived on earth and been "crucified under Pontius Pilate."

The Christian thought which began with Jesus was exploring thus unrestingly the dimensions of its faith. To what measure had the ultimate meaning of God been revealed in him? The time was long past when he could have been thought of as only another and greater prophet, a teacher of truth about God which was bounded by time and circumstance. Could it be believed instead that in Jesus Christ men had seen the inmost reality of what God eternally is? Paul was answering *yes* to that supreme question when in the dramatic language of his letter to the Philippians he pictured the Jesus who had lived a human life of

[4] *Against Heresies,* Bk. V, Preface.
[5] *Exhortation to the Heathen,* ch. 2.

79

service as having had in heaven equality with God. And when Origen at the beginning of the third century taught "the eternal generation of the Son," he was using the language of the philosophers, but back of his words was the conviction that the everlasting purpose of the Father was and is revealed in Christ.

This was the conviction to which many had been led. In the fourth century it would crystalize into a creed.

VIII

THE NICENE CREED

IT WAS IN A.D. 325 AT NICAEA, NEAR CONSTANTINOPLE, THAT the first formal creed for Christendom was shaped. After a struggle with rival claimants, the young Constantine had won the imperial power; and to the degree at least of his limited comprehension, he had become a Christian. No doubt he had political motives when he summoned some three hundred bishops to meet at Nicaea. He wanted them to agree on a statement of faith that could be an influence for unity in the empire. But also he may have had the honest, and more humble, desire to understand better what he was supposed to believe. At any rate, he did bring together the assembly which was destined to have great importance for the development of Christian doctrine.

In certain respects, the Council of Nicaea was not something to be proud of. Those who met there were presumably men of God, but their debates were filled with all-too-human acrimony. For two months, what must often have seemed to be confused and profitless disputation went on. Yet the shortcomings, both in thought and temper, of the men who gathered at Nicaea must not obscure the earnestness of conviction which made them defend their varying conceptions with such heated loyalty. The crucial question was as to how to conceive the relationship between God the Father and the Christ who had been man. The intellectual difficulty immediately arising was a double one. To begin with, there was the philosophical problem of how the infinite and all-sufficient God could create a new aspect of his own life without indicating thereby that he in himself had not been complete. How could there be Father *and* Son; and if there was the Son, the "Second Person" in the Godhead, how could he be other than secondary and subordinate? And, also, there was the further and more concrete problem of how the high God could stoop to relationship with the life of the sinful earth. One was a problem concerning God's inmost nature; the other was the problem of an incarnation.

There was the type of thought which had been represented in the middle of the third century by Dionysius, Bishop of Alexandria, who maintained that

the Son of God is a creature . . . in essence alien from the Father, just as the husbandman is from the vine, or the shipbuilder from the boat, for that, being a creature, He was not before He came to be.[1]

It was also the type of thought of Theodotus of Byzantium (at the end of the second century) who insisted that Christ was only a man on whom the Holy Spirit had descended at his baptism. But most important for the Council of Nicaea was the presbyter Arius. He did not use the extreme language of Dionysius or Theodotus, but he was moved by the same concern which affected them: a fear lest the glory of God the creator should seem diminished if it were affirmed that the Word made flesh was an equal with the Almighty. He taught that in the beginning, which was before all time, only the Creator existed, that Christ was not a part of the Godhead until he was generated by an act of the Father's will, and that when he was created he must have been subordinate. So in the debates at Nicaea the followers of

[1] Athanasius, *On the Opinion of Dionysius,* ch. 4.

Arius made one word their rallying point. In the creed that was to be shaped they wanted to say that the Church's belief in Jesus Christ was belief in one who was *homoiousios* with the Father. That is to say, he was of *like* substance with God.

Emerging at Nicaea as the voice that interpreted another view was Athanasius. Like so many others who had been influential in Christian thinking, he also came from Alexandria. At the time of the Council he was only a deacon, although later he was to become a bishop—through times of hardship and danger that would reveal in him an extraordinary moral heroism. He believed that what the Arians would have been satisfied to have the creed express could be religiously disastrous. To allow—either by what the creed should say or fail to say—the Arian suggestion that there was a time when Christ was not could mean that the redeemingness in God was an afterthought, and Christ a sort of demigod such as the Gnostic philosophers had represented him. Origen's doctrine of "the eternal generation of the Son" seemed to Athanasius to be no inconsequential metaphysical subtlety, but a truth to be reflected in the creed in the affirmation concerning Jesus Christ that he was "not made," but "begotten of his Father before all worlds." Those words should mean that the saving grace which men had known in Jesus was the everlasting mercy of the eternal God. For the same reason Athanasius resisted the adoption of the Arian word *homoiousios*. To say that Christ the Redeemer, was *like* the Father would be to say by inference that there were aspects in which he was *not* like the Father. Then there would be no sure ground of faith and trust that in what Jesus was there has been revealed what God eternally is. Therefore, Athanasius urged that in the creedal declaration concerning Jesus the word should be not *"homoiousios"* but *"homoousios,"* not of *like* substance but of *one* substance with the Father. For—as he was afterwards to write—"Beholding the Son, we see the Father; for the thought and comprehension of the Son is knowledge concerning the Father, for He is His proper offspring from His essence." [2]

At the Council of Nicaea Athanasius' thought prevailed, and the word he championed was written into the Nicene Creed. But the divisions manifest in the council were still unhealed, and for more than a century afterwards there was conflict, sometimes embittered, between those who accepted the creed and the unpersuaded Arians. Among students who have read the lam_ntable history of those years there must have been some who have been tempted to exclaim, "A plague on both your houses!" Were vital religious values really at stake beneath the clouds of controversy, thick with what may appear from this distance to have been only the dust of philosophical abstractions? Did it really matter whether the creed that was shaped should speak of Jesus Christ as *homoiousios,* or *homoousios,* with God the Father?

It is possible to feel at first impression that at Nicaea the great truths had been almost lost in abstract terminology. Even such a theologian as A. M. Fairbairn could say of some of the thinking at Nicaea that "metaphysics had triumphed over ethics, scholastic terms over moral realities." [3] Nevertheless, what the men of that council were expressing in the debate concerning *homoiousious* and *homoousios* did greatly matter—for that time; and, in the heart of what was striven for, for all times. It is true that the Hellenic terms into which the thought of that fourth century was poured are not the forms which a later generation

[2] *Discourses Against the Arians,* ch. 5.
[3] *The Place of Christ in Modern Theology* (New York: Charles Scribner's Sons, 1893), p. 91.

finds instinctive. What the men of Nicaea said may have to be reinterpreted and newly expressed; but what they were trying at length to affirm was a conviction that those who would hold to a life-giving gospel can never afford to lose. Arianism might have undercut a religious certainty that was deeper and more important than any seeming logic. To separate the Christ spirit in any manner from the eternal God could mean—as in Gnosticism—that Christ was only one of many mediators and therefore only a partial revelation of what God is. So might be lost the living conviction of the New Testament—that the one sure way by which men can come to the light and life that are of God is "through Jesus Christ our Lord."

It may be truly perceived and said concerning the Council of Nicaea that the most important fact about it was that the *living conviction* did prove stronger than philosophical complexities. In sheer logical process developed from abstract premises Arianism might have seemed entitled to prevail. But in the thought of Athanasius there was the unshakable perception that it was not an a priori assumption about the nature of God, but the fact of God as actually experienced through Christ, that is the ground of truth. Long before the term was coined, Athanasius was thinking existentially. He was saying that the minds and souls of Christians who would try to glimpse the glory of God must begin from that contact with his reality, which they already knew. In so doing, Athanasius "could appeal to age-long Christian piety," [4] for

we must remember that the primary purpose of the Nicene theology was religious rather than philosophical. When Christians say that

[4] A. C. McGiffert, *The God of the Early Christians* (New York: Charles Scribner's Sons, 1925), p. 99.

Christ was "God of God, Light of Light, very God of very God" and "of one substance with the Father," they are testifying that he who has brought redemption and new life to themselves and countless others must in some incomprehensible way have had God in him. They are asserting that God Himself has broken through the veil that separates man from Him and disclosed fully His nature as redemptive love in Jesus of Nazareth.[5]

The reality expressed in those words is what always constituted the heart of Athanasius' thinking. In his theology "there is argument, reasoning, searching for proof and their statement"; but, as T. M. Lindsay has gone on to say:

All that belongs to the outworks in his teaching. The central citadel is a spiritual intuition—I *know* that *my* Saviour is the God Who made heaven and earth. He took his stand firmly and unflinchingly on that personal experience, and all else mattered little compared with the fundamental spiritual fact. It was not his arguments, but his unflinching faith, that convinced his generation.[6]

The problems of thought which confronted the men of Nicaea were not peculiar to their time. They may recur in the intellectual questioning of every age. As to the first aspect of difficulty, the philosophical problem of how the Absolute can become also the Related and specifically, therefore, how the infinite God could be made manifest in Jesus, Cyril Richardson has forthrightly recognized that there is no theoretical solution. "All we can say is that God is *both*, and leave it at that." [7] By "leave

[5] George F. Thomas in *The Christian Answer*, ed. Henry P. Van Dusen (New York: Charles Scribner's Sons, 1945), p. 114. By permission.

[6] *A History of the Reformation* (New York: Charles Scribner's Sons, 1906), I, 433.

[7] *Op. cit.*, p. 43.

it at that," he means, of course, that in the greatness of God there are actualities so wide that they may be to us a paradox— a paradox which nevertheless must be accepted, because to try to escape it would be to lose a part of the living fact. And he goes on to say:

He is these two things; he exists in these two modes of being— but neither is prior to the other. In no sense can we say he is *first* the all-glorious, and *then* is able to be related to his creation. His capacity for action is not secondary to his absolute character. In one of the most thorough and serious attempts recently to deal with the Trinity, Karl Barth posits the difference between Father and Son in terms of God's revelation. . . . that in revelation God distinguishes himself from himself. It is his property "hiddenly to be God and yet at the same time and in quite another way, namely, manifestly, i.e. in the form of something He Himself is not, to be God a second time." The distinction between Father and Son is that between God as veiled and God as unveiled. This is a way of putting the basic distinction we have made between God in his beyondness and God in his relatedness. But Barth makes the second dependent upon the first. And why? Because he assumes that God by his nature *"cannot be unveiled to man,"* and hence in revelation has to become "God a second time." But this assumption is unwarranted. We have no reason for claiming that God by his nature is such that, *first,* he cannot be unveiled to man, and so has to make himself God a *second* time, as if the first mode of his being were the prior one. All we are justified in saying is that God by his nature exists in these two modes, unveiled and veiled, related and beyond. But that one is prior to the other in any sense cannot be assumed. All we can assume is that as absolutely beyond, God *cannot* be unveiled to man but that as related, he *can.* It is his character to be both; and he is not more God or "first" God one way or the other.[8]

[8] *Ibid.,* pp. 36-37.

It is told of that brilliant scholar at the General Seminary in New York, Burton S. Easton, that when he had been lecturing on some profound theme, he might look up in his abrupt manner and throw out the challenge, "Now, gentlemen, is that clear?" And if anyone incautiously raised his hand and indicated that, yes, it was clear, Easton would answer, "If you think it is clear, then you have it wrong." The need of that sort of wholesome warning can certainly be recognized in connection with the logical difficulties which the men of Nicaea confronted. The general problem of how the Absolute could become the Related was difficult enough; and so far as philosophical theory was concerned, the difficulty was doubled when it was declared that the presence of God had come into the actual world in the man of whom it was scornfully asked, "Can any good thing come out of Nazareth?" If God is infinite and ineffable, how could he be revealed within the compass of a human life that ended on a cross?

But exactly out of that accentuated problem came the revolutionary answer. It involved a whole new frame of reference, and a new premise from which thinking would begin. That premise was the *fact* of what had come into the world in Christ. Christian men and women, whether learned or unlearned, knew that through him they had been given a new sense of the nearness of God and of a saving love that reached out to them redeemingly even in their sinfulness and would not let them go.

This reality of experience, and not old preconceptions of philosophy about the supposed hidden nature of an unknowable God, should be the starting point of the living truth. The theologians would have to devise the best language they could by which to express it, but the supreme thing to be expressed was the certainty that God the Father could be known through God the Son. Philosophers might have their problems as to how this could be, but that is the way it *was*. Henceforth all conceptions of God must be shaped in that ultimate light which had shone in the life of Jesus.

The more thoughtfully one considers the Nicene Creed and the essential belief which was seeking expression through its form, the more closely it can stand related to thinking and questioning which are real today.

When the Nicene Creed proclaimed its faith that the "one Lord Jesus Christ" had been "begotten of his Father before all worlds," it was saying something which helps to answer perplexities which continually recur.

There is—for one thing—the perplexity as to the relationship of Christian faith to the whole of history. Often someone asks: What happened in the times before the Incarnation? If the full revelation of God came only in Jesus Christ, then were all those who lived and died before him left without saving light?

No; and in the illumination of the Nicene faith the perplexity begins to clear. From all eternity there has been, so to speak, the Christness in God, which is to say that God's essential nature is creative love, and that this creative love which chose to fashion souls that could look up to him has been the everlasting Word, which in every generation has spoken to men in the measure of their understanding and response. That was what Clement of Alexandria had believed, and what he had taught could be summed up thus:

Christ is the Light that broods over all history, and lighteth every man that cometh into the world. All that there is upon earth of beauty, truth, goodness, all that distinguishes the civilized man from the savage, the savage from the beasts, is His gift.[9]

From this same Word of God there has come to the great spirits among various peoples that which made them great and good, as to Jeremiah in Jerusalem, to Buddha in India, to Socrates in Greece.

And, as F. R. Barry has written:

Christianity has never taught that Christ is the only revelation of God. . . . The very presence of the Old Testament bound up in our Bibles with the Christian scriptures is standing witness to this contention. . . . The whole Christian faith is really meaningless unless we conceive God's work in Christ in relation to the whole sweep and range of God's work throughout the cosmic process.[10]

What the Christian faith does say is that in Jesus the light of the meaning of God which had been reflected partially here and there shone at length unclouded and complete. "The Word was made flesh, and dwelt among us." (John 1:14.)

But if that be said, then it could be asked—as it sometimes is—how does Jesus differ from other great spiritual figures except in degree? And if he has brought God to men only in larger degree, then in what sense can he be looked to as uniquely the Lord of life?

Concerning that, though no attempted answer from our finite knowledge can be sufficient, a homely simile may be suggestive. Consider what happens when water is set above a flame. As the radiation from the fire penetrates it, the water grows increasingly hot. Still there is no startling difference. Little by little the heat

[9] Charles Bigg, *The Christian Platonists of Alexandria* (New York: Oxford University Press, 1886), p. 72.
[10] *The Relevance of Christianity* (London: Nisbet & Co., 1931), p. 161.

rises in degree, but the water is still only hot water. But then there comes the decisive point where something crucial happens. The water turns into steam. The difference now might be said to be only a further difference in degree, but it is also a difference in kind. The water that was static has become creative energy, and in that transformation makes possible what was never possible before.

So, if only in far-off similitude, the presence of God in the human Jesus may be conceived. To think of God as "substance" may no longer fit into our thought, as it did into Hellenic thinking, and shape the particular language of the creed; but think of God as Spirit, and then the analogy just suggested may have a living meaning. If the mind and will of Jesus were completely permeated and possessed by the redeeming purpose which is the heart of God's reality, then there was in him the dynamic difference from all the rest of mankind which made him "very God of very God." [11]

This actual and living fact that Jesus represented and communicated what Tillich calls the New Being, was the deep realization which was trying to find expression in the creeds. That was true at Nicaea; it was true also—notwithstanding its more in-

[11] After the manuscript of this book had been completed and was in the hands of the publishers, there appeared W. Norman Pittenger's *The Word Incarnate*, an interpretation of exceeding value both for its scholarliness and for its religious warmth. In it, beginning on page 188, one can read these sentences: "The question may arise whether this conception of our Lord as the 'en-manned Word' means that he is different only in degree from the other instances of the Word's operative presence. . . . I believe that in one sense the dilemma 'degree or kind' is a false dilemma . . . Deity wherever found is deity, not 'more' or 'less' divine; but there is of course a difference in what we may call the 'intensity' of the divine operation. . . . We can say that the intensity of the operation of God in union with the humanity of Jesus is so great, as demonstrated by its concrete results, that he is God-man rather than God 'acting in' a man."

volved and labored language—in the creed drawn up by the Council or Chalcedon in 451. That council declared:

Following therefore the holy Fathers, we confess one and the same our Lord Jesus Christ, and we all teach harmoniously [that he is] the same perfect in Godhead, the same perfect in manhood, truly God and truly man, the same of a reasonable soul and body; consubstantial with the Father in Godhead, and the same consubstantial with us in manhood, like us in all things except sin; . . . acknowledged in two natures without confusion, without change, without division, without separation.[12]

For that council, the problem was how to express what men had found in Jesus, the unity of what was completely human with that which was completely divine. As the Nicene Creed had used the thought-form of oneness in "substance," the Creed of Chalcedon tried to embody the same conviction in terms of divine and human "nature."

Any diminution of the human nature would deprive the Christ of his total participation in the conditions of existence. And any diminution of the divine nature would deprive the Christ of his total victory over existential estrangement.[13]

The problem of expressing in language the fullness of the meaning of Christ "never has been solved adequately, even within the limits of human possibilities." But at Nicea and at Chalcedon, "both the Christ-character and the Jesus-character of the event of Jesus as the Christ were preserved." [14] To say this is to remember what was always the supreme effort of the creeds: not

[12] *Library of Christian Classics* (Philadelphia: The Westminster Press, 1954), Vol. III.
[13] Paul Tillich, *op. cit.*, II, 142.
[14] *Ibid.*, p. 145.

to devise definitions for their own sake but, in spite of the imperfection of all definitions, to proclaim the dynamic faith that through Jesus Christ men find new life in God.

Donald Baillie, with his rich combination of scholarly learning and spiritual insight, has dealt with what he calls "the paradox of grace and the paradox of the Incarnation." Everyone who thinks of the great saints of Christendom will be confronted in the record of their lives with the paradox of grace; and every humble Christian can know its reality in himself. He feels, on the one hand, his own moral freedom and responsibility as a human being. He himself must be seeking God, and he himself must be choosing goodness. But on the other hand, he understands more and more the everlasting truth of what Paul wrote: "It is God which worketh in you both to will and to do of his good pleasure" (Phil. 2:13). All that one has of aspiration and achievement is not of one's own invention. It is the response of the soul to the heavenly grace which does not destroy or dim the human self, but lifts it toward the fullness of what essentially it was meant to be. So Donald Baillie writes,

The whole experience of this paradox, which covers only those fragments of our lives in which there is something good, has come into our lives through One in whom it covered the whole of His life, so that His life was the very life of God himself, and yet was at the same time in the fullest sense the life of a man. Jesus Christ is the One in whom human selfhood fully came to its own and lived its fullest life, as human life ought to be lived, because His human selfhood was wholly yielded to God, so that His whole life was the life of God. That was the one life which was wholly Divine and wholly human.[15]

[15] *God Was in Christ* (New York: Charles Scribner's Sons, 1948), p. 145. Used by permission of Charles Scribner's Sons and Faber and Faber, Ltd.

It is important that in those words there should be no confusion as to emphasis and priority. To say that "his human selfhood was wholly yielded to God" must never be understood as suggesting that the dynamic which made Jesus what he was came first from the human side—as though the Man of Nazareth first reached up toward the Divine, until at length he touched it. The profundity of Christian faith is that the initiative came from the infinite Reality. The life of Jesus, with its beauty of perfect holiness and its unbounded redeeming love, was and is the coming-near of God.

The Nicene Creed, in its symbolic language, expresses the eternal spiritual truth when it speaks of him "Who for us men and for our salvation came down from heaven." In him we have more than an exemplar whom we in our human frailty would despair of being fit even to try to follow. The closer we come in thought and commitment to the spirit of Jesus, the more we become aware of Him whom Jesus called "My Father and your Father," and the more sure that the heavenly love itself is reaching down to what otherwise would be our lostness and aloneness.

In the Nicene Creed, even in forms of expression the relevance of which we may not quickly see, there is a relationship to another question that is often reaching out for answer. We say as Christians that we find the meaning of God supremely in Jesus. But there are those who ask: How much do we really know of Jesus? And how much can we know? Are some of our conceptions of him just our own ideas projected back and made imagined fact? How can we take our guidance from a figure too hidden in the far past for us to say honestly that we understand him, or understand what his pattern for our lives would be?

The answer is that it is not only from the historic records that we can know Christ. The Nicene Creed speaks of him as "be-

gotten of his Father before all worlds," and it proclaims the Holy
Ghost as the Spirit "who proceedeth from the Father and the
Son." To say those words is to remember that what was revealed
of God in Jesus has been true forever, and that the light of God
that was in him has proceeded from him through the Spirit to be
an awareness in us now. Late in the fourth century the Christian thinkers known as the Cappadocian fathers set forth the
doctrine of *Circumincessio,* meaning, "a proceeding around."
Though that term may sound remote, it expresses what all human souls—not the theologically learned only—can experience
every day as real. For it means that every aspect in which we
know God illumines, and is illumined by, every other aspect in
which he might be known.

We read the Gospels and try again to see the figure of Jesus
as it is pictured there. But we are not left with that alone. In
one's own soul there is the immediate witness that speaks of him.
There is a voice within the consciousness of every man which
makes him aware of what is Christlike. Even though he may
try to ignore that voice, he registers what it is saying. He may
have had little explicit thought of Christ and may not call himself a Christian. But when he searches his soul, what does he
acknowledge? A recognition of what life *ought* to be and at its
best *would* be. He knows that the real man in him cannot live
by bread alone, that life grows mean and sour when it is selfish
and is lifted to greatness only when it risks a costly loyalty to
some great cause.

The reason he knows this is because the Holy Spirit "who
proceedeth from the Father and the Son" has entered him, no
matter if he did not know its name. Then if one day he begins
to think of the figure of Jesus, he will understand him better
because of the intimations in his own soul; and at the same time

his own conceptions of goodness become subject to the objective standard that he sees in Jesus, and measured by their likeness or their unlikeness to him. In the end God the Father—God in his infiniteness and profundity—is trusted as having been revealed both by the Holy Spirit in the heart and by Jesus Christ to whom that Spirit points.

IX

LIVING
CONSEQUENCES OF THE CREED

THE PRECEDING CHAPTER, ESPECIALLY IN ITS CONCLUDING paragraphs, had to do with a question and with the beginning of its answer.

What is the nature of God?—that is what human souls most deeply need to know. And the answer that the Council of Nicaea dared to give was supremely this: that he is such a God as was revealed in the Incarnation.

Henry Sloane Coffin used to say that the doctrine of the deity of Jesus is not so much a doctrine about Jesus as it is a doctrine about God. The first disciples looked at Jesus, and something happened to their feeling and to their thought concerning God. It was not, of course, that they only then began to believe in God. By inheritance and sure conviction they shared the agelong faith of Israel: faith in the eternal Lord of history, creator and sustainer of all things, who in his holy purpose had made a covenant of promise for his people. In the supreme hours of the nation's life, and as a surety in its crises, Israel had believed in the *shekinah,* the presence of God that was forever with his people and guided them so certainly that in the great record of the exodus from Egypt it could be remembered as like a pillar of cloud by day and of fire by night. This trust in the divine protection which forever overshadowed the people of the covenant could produce, and did produce, souls of deep piety and spiritual power. But it was possible also for humble men and women to think of the God of Israel as concerned most with a nation's destiny: a God of awful majesty known in the deliverance from Egypt, in the thunder clouds of Sinai, and in the giving of the law. Such may have been the instinctive feeling of the ordinary folk who led what might have seemed their insignificant lives in Galilee. But when they came into contact with Jesus they had a new experience. "The one true God of the old Jewish faith, the God of Abraham, Isaac and Jacob, had now acted in a new way. What was involved was not (so to speak) an enlargement of God, but an enlargement of man's revealed knowledge of God." [1] The God whom Jesus called "My Father and your Father" was their same God, but revealed now in a different light. Looking at Jesus, they believed more than they ever had before that God cared *for them*. Because of Jesus, they would see the meaning of God henceforth as through Jesus' eyes. And this is what they saw: a righteousness relentless in its challenge; a condemnation of all that is small and mean; a hold upon men's souls that will not let them rest until they have seen and striven toward the highest; yet this not in the mood of judgment but in the redeeming compassion of a love that must show men their faults and sins in order to set them free. Such is the conception of God that has always come through Jesus; and to say that Jesus is "God of God, Light of Light, Very God of very God. . . . Being of one substance with the Father" is to say that the one whom he called his Father is no other than what the Jesus of the Gospels made men trust that God must be.

To hold to that is to be at the heart of the Christian faith.

---

[1] Alan Richardson, *An Introduction to the Theology of the New Testament* (New York: Harper & Brothers, 1958), p. 122.

Various distortions of thought in the first three Christian centuries tended to lead men away from it; modern distortions of thought could lead us away from it today.

In the Greco-Roman world there were many who were dominated by the Platonic thought of God as dwelling in the realm of pure idea, the purity of which could not be expressed—and must never be regarded as entangled—in the world of the concrete and the material. Consequently, teachers like those of the Gnostic schools had to evolve a long chain of intermediaries to separate the absolute God from contact with human life.

Nor was it only the influences that came from Hellenic philosophy that made men shrink from belief in an actual incarnation of the Divine. There were some inheritances from the Old Testament that had the same effect. The awful majesty of God must not be diminished. He whose sacredness was such that even his name must not be spoken—how could he be said to be present in a man moving among men? So Arius, constrained by what to him was a logic as reverent as it was irresistible, maintained that Jesus Christ could not be of one substance with the Father; there must be a separation and a difference.

On the basis of logical argument and of long accepted thinking, Arius seemed to be right, and to the minds of many he *was* right. But in Athanasius and in those who followed him, as we have seen, there was an instinctive awareness of something new, something bigger than philosophical consistency and more dynamic than old theological forms. Arius and those who agreed with him began with a priori orthodoxies as to what must be the nature of the absolute God. But the Nicene Creed, as Athanasius helped to shape it, dared to take as its central ground what seemed the incredible, but all the same was the actual, fact—that the very reality of God had been revealed in Jesus. From *this* starting

99

point and not from the other, from what had been *shown* to men in Jesus and not from even the most accepted previous speculations into the unknown, must the truth be seen. The Incarnation was the focus through which the utmost that men could understand of God would be brought into view. What belief in the Incarnation has to say to actual life is this: stand in imagination where the disciples stood, feel those convictions which they felt as life got its meaning for them through Jesus—living, crucified, and alive again—and then a man can believe with them that when he looks into the Infinite—whatever be its present hidden depths—there will be nothing in all the greatness of God that will be unlike what men have experienced in the redeeming Christ. The language of the Nicene Creed may seem antiquated, and the patterns of its expression not our instinctive patterns; but its power is in the vital religious meaning which everlastingly burns through its words.

As this religious meaning might have been eclipsed by other types of thinking in the early Church, so there is real danger that some contemporary theological influences now may obscure aspects of the divine Reality which, if forgotten, would impoverish Christian faith and life. Specifically, that can be true of the neo-orthodoxy of Barth and Brunner and others of their school.

To say that does not mean anything so shallow as disparagement of the signal contributions which this momentous theological trend has brought to Christian interpretations of God and man. It has humbled human pride, the pride both of pretended knowledge and of moral presumption. It has deepened the consciousness of the rebellion and estrangement from God which runs like a dark river through so much of human life.

If men are to be redeemed, they need to be made conscious

of that estrangement; they need to know why it is that under the surface of apparent satisfactions they may be haunted by a hollow discontent. Many men may have to learn what was learned by Francis Gaillard in John Buchan's *Mountain Meadow*. He fled from the world of his success to go back to the harsh frontier country whose loyalties he thought he had betrayed, because "he had forgtten something of desperate importance, his eternal welfare." " 'I came to realise that I had forgotten God,' he said simply." [2]

So, as against a glib little humanism and a shallow hunt for happiness, neo-orthodoxy has faced this generation with the imperious message that it remember God. Man stands under the eternal judgment; and until one reckons with that truth, the soul's evasions can end in nothing but inner division and unrest. There is a divine pursuit, as by the "Hound of Heaven," which the soul cannot escape.

But what is the nature and character of God who thus confronts the soul—in judgment first, but not *for* judgment; rather, to redeem and save? It is when that question is asked that there may be revealed in neo-orthodoxy aspects which need to be regarded with grave concern. The important field for that concern is not in theological theory; it is in the conceptions of God which affect actual people's everyday living and may make the difference for their spirit between encouragement and depression, if not between encouragement and despair.

To Karl Barth, according to the flat statement which one finds in his early writing, God must be thought of as the "Wholly Other." Emil Brunner has written: "He reveals himself as the

[2] (Boston: Houghton Mifflin Co., 1940), pp. 206, 207.

unheard-of, unrecognized mysterious person, who cannot be discovered anywhere in the world." [3]

If those words were taken to be baldly true, the consequence for many ordinary people might be the chilled idea that God is not within the real life they have to lead. If they want to know God, there is no use looking for him—so they must suppose—in the familiar or the near. But if they can never see a religious meaning breaking through the life around them, how will they ever gain a consciousness of God? Perhaps the theological professionals can have a transcendent revelation; but can *they*?

Later expressions both of Barth and, especially, of Brunner have seemed to modify the utter repudiation of any instinctive awareness of God in human souls which the words above conveyed. But the full result of a theological movement is represented not only by those whose living thought first launches it, but also by the multitude of listeners and imitators who plunge into the current of the new thinking and follow it with blind intensity of commitment. Of the creative mind it can be true, as Paul Tillich has said about Barth, that "Barth's greatness is that he corrects himself again and again in the light of the 'situation' and that he strenuously tries not to become his own follower";[4] but the lesser disciples of neo-orthodoxy have often had no such flexibility. They have preached—and still may preach—an almost fanatical denial of any image of God still present in man, the ultimate hopelessness of all human activity, and such instinctive belittlement of everything in the human sphere that interest in the life and words of the actual Jesus disappears in dog-

[3] *The Theology of Crisis* (New York: Charles Scribner's Sons, 1935), p. 33.

[4] Quoted by H. E. Fosdick, *The Living of These Days* (New York: Harper & Brothers, 1956), p. 249.

matisms concerning a wholly metaphysical Christ.[5] These spokesmen for what they proclaim as neo-orthodoxy are right in their conviction that man can never be saved by his own devices but only by the grace of God; but their error lies in the harsh exclusiveness which refuses to recognize the wideness of the ways in which that grace may actually come. When Reinhold Niebuhr, on the other hand, presents the desperate state of man,

> he is provocative, stimulating, shocking, challenging, sometimes paradoxically bewildering, but he is not disheartening. He comes at us, like Winston Churchill, with a message of "blood, toil, tears, and sweat," not to dismay but to arouse. Some of the neo-orthodox, however, especially some of the camp-followers, do vilify man in order to glorify God, reducing man to mere emptiness and impotence.[6]

When neo-orthodoxy arrives at that point it has become, not a Christian message, but a Christian heresy. Carried out to its full implications, it can involve a bleak denial of the central message of the Incarnation. If God were indeed the "Wholly Other," then we should be turned back to a kind of Gnostic theophany in which God's communication of himself to man becomes a process unintelligible to the ordinary mind, and paralyzing—like arctic cold—to the instinctive hope which men's everyday experiences can make them feel.

[5] And as precedent for such twist of thought, there could be cited words of Brunner himself, who had written: "How Jesus found God, how he prayed, how he lived, is not divine revelation for us" (*The Theology of Crisis*, p. 36); "The Christian faith has just as little to do with the influence of Jesus on the history of the world as it has to do with his historical personality. It is not interested in the 'Founder of Christianity,' nor in his influence on history" (*The Mediator*, p. 81); "Jesus as an epoch-making personality is—like all other world history—dust, mortality" (*Our Faith*, p. 58); "The 'historical Jesus' is a corpse, a scientific abstraction which is of no value to us" (*The Word and the World*, p. 88.)

[6] Harry E. Fosdick, *op. cit.*, p. 252.

As neo-orthodoxy has brought again the awesome and purifying message of God's transcendence, its pendulum has swung so far in that direction that it has lost the truth that God, in his purpose of redemption, can actually be always coming near. In its drastic chastening of human vanity this theology may obscure the points of contact at which God touches man in what the best in man still knows and feels.

The gospel of the Incarnation, as H. R. Mackintosh has written in *The Doctrine of the Person of Jesus Christ,* implies that because God made man in his own image, therefore, man in his God-given nature is susceptible of God. "To assume an ultimate dualism in this sphere is to condemn the Christologian to failure from the start." Then Mackintosh adds to his own expression these words from J. Caird's *Fundamental Ideas:*

If our notions of divinity and humanity contain heterogeneous or contradictory elements, it is a truism to say that we can no more combine them in the conception of one and the same personality than we can think of a square circle, or a quadrilateral triangle, or a straight circle[7]

Mackintosh goes on:

In the view of Scripture there is no such inherent disparity between the Divine and human as to make their union inconceivable. . . . Man is the son of God, even if a lost son; and it is his proper destiny to be partaker of the divine life.[8]

The great worth of the neo-orthodox message, as we have recognized, is that it demolishes, as with a relentless wind, the cheap and pretentious self-assurance in which the generation

[7] (New York: Chas. Scribner's Sons, 1912), p. 439.
[8] *Ibid.,* p. 434.

before the two world wars had thought that life could establish itself. It brings home the imperious truth that ultimate security can only be in God, and that men can find salvation only as they turn to him. But the error comes when propagandists of the newly seized ideas, with an obsessive overemphasis, make it appear not only that man can never be sufficient in himself, but that nothing man can do, and nothing that he can experience except in some directly supernatural unearthliness, can give significance to his common day. Instead, "The Eternal came into the temporal, 'not to destroy but to fulfil,'" writes Leonard Hodgson in *The Doctrine of the Trinity*. Referring to "some exponents of the Barthian movement, and of Rudolf Otto's theory of the numinous," he goes on to say:

They emphasise the gulf between Creator and created, between God and man, between Eternal and temporal. The practical conclusion which they draw for religion is that man should acknowledge the utter worthlessness of his earthly life, and bow himself in uncomprehending awe before the *mysterium fascinosum tremendum*. But such religion is emphatically not historic Christianity. Historic Christianity . . . is the acceptance of the adopted sonship of God in Christ, the realisation of a vocation to the status of co-worker in creation. The depth of the richness of the Divine Being may be such that He will always be to us the *mysterium fascinosum tremendum*, but it need never again be the utterly impenetrable mystery of a *wholly* other. The godhead may be that to men who stand and gaze upon it, so to speak, from without; but we have been taken within, to look out upon the world around us with "the mind of Christ." Hence the Christian doctrine of God contains the corrective both of human arrogance and of its obscurantist antidote.[9]

[9] Hodgson, *op. cit.*, p. 65.

"The status of co-worker in creation": it is the inspiration of this possibility that extreme neo-orthodoxy may extinguish like a candle blown out in a wintry draught. The Incarnation means that human life as such may be the medium through which God's meaning shines. To forget that is to cut existence in two and to assume that the only persons who can know the truth of God are those who are studying books that are most emphatic about his being far away. So there happens what can actually be seen: the gulf of separation between the academically religious and people who go about their ordinary work. The minister or the student in the seminary may seem to have channels of spiritual communication which the student's wife does not possess. She moves in her routine of inconspicuous duties: every morning straightening up a house, getting breakfast ready, feeding a baby; then errands to the grocery store, dinner to cook when she hurries back, a quick visit to carry some flowers to a neighbor who has been sick, and a few of the flowers on the table to make the living room look bright when her husband comes home at the end of the day. How will all this connect with what her husband has been hearing of God as the "Wholly Other" and of "the utter worthlessness" of this human life?

But the fact is that all the while the girl who has been reading no neo-orthodoxy may have had the heavenly Reality singing in her heart: the Reality which Jesus saw reflected in the nesting of birds, in the kneading of the leaven into the meal, in the shepherd caring for the sheep. "I come in the little things, saith the Lord": not in the great wind, or the fire, but in the still, small voice. The cup poured for a thirsty child in the unself-conscious service of the common day may become, according to the words of Jesus, "a spring of water welling up to eternal life" (John 4:14).

Such can be some of the corollaries of the Incarnation. It is not the far-off holiness but self-giving love that saves. When we remember *this* we come closest to the Christian faith as to what is the meaning of God.

That is the faith that men would like to hold. If it is so, then the universe is not empty, and at its center is one to whom even the least soul is not insignificant and on whose strength and grace we can rely.

But can we actually hold to that conviction? The Nicene Creed proclaims the fullness of the Incarnation, which means that Jesus is the complete interpreter of God, and that God in his infinity is the same unfailing goodness that the disciples knew in Jesus when they loved and trusted him. But the creed itself seems to embody a contradiction. The Jesus who is professed as "God of God" and "Light of light" nevertheless "suffered and was buried." Was it all an illusion, then, that the unseen is what Jesus was—an illusion of projecting into the unknown an unsupported longing that there may be a God as good as human hearts have wistfully imagined and desired? Suffering and sorrow; disappointment, seeming defeat, and death; bewilderment of the mind and a dark night of the soul—all these belong among the harsh and inescapable facts of actual existence.

There is no way of waving some wand of sentimentalism and pretending that the harsh facts disappear. It is naïve and ignorant to suppose that Christian faith must deny the reality of disorder and of evil. The real world is no "child's landscape, filled with ladies, bunnies, fairies, and harmless men with clerical collars," and wherever the vapid notion spreads that the world is such, then Christianity would lose its power and relevance to the problems of life. "No wonder those people who live immersed within the tragedies of existence, amid its real frustra-

107

tion; and insecurities, its deep conflicts of power, and its inescapable sufferings, are offended by the falsity of this picture ... and suspect that those who hold it find in this sentimentalism a helpful excuse for doing nothing about the world's various ills." [10]

But when sentimentalism is laid aside and the harsh realities confronted, some may be troubled and uncertain. They have a wistful longing for a positive faith and an impulse to cry out, "Lord, I believe"; yet a restraining honesty makes them know that the best they can say is, "Help thou my unbelief!" Franklin K. Lane, one of the secretaries in the cabinet of President Woodrow Wilson, wrote to a friend:

I am trying hard to believe something that might be called the shadow of a religion—a God that has a good purpose, and another life in which there is a chance for further growth, if not for glory. But when I bump up against a series of afflictions such as you have been subjected to, I fall back upon the philosophy of a purposeless or else a cruel God. . . . I simply have a sinking of the heart, a goneness, a hopelessness. "The mystical hanker after something higher" is religion, and yet it should not be all of religion; for man's own sake there should be some cross to which one can cling, some Christ who can hear and give peace to the waves." [11]

Typical of some in every generation are Thomas Hardy's somber lines in "God's Funeral," like mournful music lamenting the lost loveliness of an ultimate trust that for him seemed forever gone. "What we had imagined," he wrote, "we once believed." But only

[10] Langdon Gilkey, *Maker of Heaven and Earth* (Garden City, N. Y.: Doubleday and Company, 1959), p. 108.

[11] *The Letters of Franklin K. Lane* (Boston: Houghton Mifflin Co., 1922), pp. 313, 218. By permission of Nancy Lane.

Till, in Time's stayless stealthy swing,
Uncompromising rude reality
Mangled the Monarch of our fashioning,
Who quavered, sank; and now has ceased to be,

So, toward our myth's oblivion,
Darkling and languid-lipped, we creep and grope
Sadlier than those who wept in Babylon,
Whose Zion was a still abiding hope.[12]

And still more modern is the voice that comes from Archibald MacLeish's *J.B.*, the poetic drama which re-enacts in contemporary terms the immemorial tragedy of inexplicable human suffering which was represented long ago in the book of Job. The figure in that drama who, going up and down in the earth, has seen the injustice and the seeming irrationality of life, chants mockingly:

> I heard upon his dry dung heap
> That man cry out who cannot sleep;
> "If God is God He is not good,
> If God is good He is not God,
> Take the even, take the odd." [13]

That figure in *J.B.* who represents the scorner's questioning of God will "take the odd." If God *is* God and therefore responsible for life with all its seeming cruelty, then he is not good; for men suffer inexplicably if God is aloof and unconcerned. This is the contradiction that challenges the would-be trust of the soul; and nothing less than the Christian creed can face that

---

[12] Reprinted from "God's Funeral" from *Collected Poems of Thomas Hardy*, by permission of The Trustees of the Hardy Estate, Macmillan & Co., Ltd., The Macmillan Company, and the Macmillan Company of Canada, Limited.
[13] (Boston: Houghton Mifflin Co., 1958). By permission.

contradiction. For the Christian sees the truth of God revealed in the life and sacrifice of Jesus. Christ on the cross has brought to human souls the everlasting conviction that out of the deepest darkness deliverance can come. The most terrible and—at its moment—the most unintelligible fact in all human history has confirmed men's faith that there can be no death or ultimate defeat for the goodness that has come from God. Christ crucified has become Christ living and inspiring.

Looking at the agony of the Cross, no one can feel alone in his own most agonizing perplexity; and looking at Christ, no one can stand bereft of faith that there will be an outcome through which the utmost that he has experienced will be glorified. He will know at length that there is no depth to which he can go down and not find God. God's love is a part of all heroic human struggle, to suffer in and with it, and to turn the temporary tragedy into spiritual triumph. The *why* of that is still a mystery, but it is a mystery at the heart of which is healing.

So, out of the shadows which fall around the spirit's search, it is the light that comes from God in Christ that can point forward. The uniqueness of Christian thought is that it must always be Christocentric at the point of the beginning from which thought moves on toward the fullness of God. From *that* center of the life, which in its transforming influence was and is "the Light of the world," all intuitions take their guidance and their sure direction. Tertullian, in his letter to Marcion,[13] referred to those who argue from the supposed attributes of a God "who is invisible and unapproachable, and placid and (so to say) the God of the philosophers," whereas the glory of the divine shines through the very facts by which to the eyes of the

[13] 2:27.

world it may seem to have been laid waste. "What in your esteem is the entire disgrace of my God," wrote Tertullian, "is in fact the pledge of man's salvation."

So it has proved in the long human experience, which is more solid than theory and stronger than abstract doubt. Men and women through all the Christian centuries who have tried to learn from Jesus have found that the way of service, even when it is a way of suffering, is the highroad that leads them up to God. Though there have been the hours when they, too, have cried, "My God, my God, why hast thou forsaken me?" they have learned that whatever be the crises of life, at the end there is the everlasting Mercy.

Genuinely to say the Nicene Creed is to affirm that faith, and to trust life to its consequences. The crucial word, be it remembered, is *faith*. Not an abstract doctrine that can be demonstrated sitting down, but the risk of action; not moorings fastened in the shallow bay of verbal statements, but the lifted sail for the ocean-wide adventure which must find its justification in the great horizons to which life can be led on. That living faith in a love which carries on the atoning love of Jesus is what the great souls have dared—a Francis of Assisi, a Wilfred Grenfell, an Albert Schweitzer, and many a Christian of lesser name— and in the inner certainty and power that came to them, they have known that what they trusted has been true.

X

THE DOCTRINE
OF THE TRINITY EMERGES

IN AN ADDRESS IN NEW YORK CITY A GOOD MANY YEARS AGO, Glenn Frank, later president of the University of Wisconsin, spoke a sentence which one of his hearers has never forgotten. Religion, as man's upreach and as the infinite answer, arises, he said, from a double need: the need "of light on the mystery of life, and strength for the mastery of life."

Sometimes men have thought that one of those needs might be satisfied without the other. Stoicism has nerved men to stand up to the tests of living even when they saw no ultimate meaning in it. William Ernest Henley, in "Invictus," could write:

> Beyond this place of wrath and tears
> Looms but the horror of the shade,
> And yet the menace of the years
> Finds, and shall find me, unafraid.

Even if life were only "the fell clutch of circumstance," he would declare,

> I am the master of my fate;
> I am the captain of my soul.

So a man may summon up his courage to go forward, although

the mystery of his existence may still seem to him "black as the pit from pole to pole."

More affirmatively, and in less somber mood, it can be urged that our business is to strive for mastery without waiting for answers to the mystery. As Dean Inge, of St. Paul's Cathedral, London, once wrote: "We cannot penetrate the mind of the Absolute"; and, going on to acknowledge that there are philosophical problems that we cannot solve, he said that there are realities "which we have to accept, not to account for." And "I see no reason why we should be admitted behind the scenes when our business is on the stage." [1]

There is truth—and it may be valiant truth—in both those attitudes. There are times when men have to act, notwithstanding that it is in the uncertainty of darkness that they must do so. But in the long run that is not enough. There is always the intuitive feeling that there is light, and that if one faces in the right direction, he will see it dawning.

It is also true that the two needs, in their expression and in their results, are not separate; they interact. The strength in men to achieve mastery depends upon at least some partial moral and spiritual illumination. When they have followed such light as they have, they grow convinced that there will be more. There cannot be a lasting mastery of life unless life has meaning in it. So there comes the inevitable longing to know what the meaning is—God's meaning, which is so great that it will always have its areas of mystery, but mystery at the center of which there must be light.

Thus it was both inevitable and right that in the Christian church there should be the increasing effort to understand and

[1] *Science and Ultimate Truth* (New York: Longmans, Green, and Co., 1926), p. 28.

to explicate the realities by which Christians had been stirred. The followers of Jesus, to whom there had come what Mark calls, "The beginning of the gospel of Jesus Christ, the Son of God" (1:1), had received something that was vital. The evangelists of the Synoptic Gospels wrote from the midst of a fellowship possessed by an experience that gave them new inspiration for their daily living. It was out of experience, certainly, that Paul wrote and preached; the same was true of John and of all the other writers of the New Testament. But men cannot be content with something that they only feel. They want to be convinced that what they feel is grounded in the everlasting truth. Could what they had tried to live by be validated in a fullness that would satisfy the mind as well as the intuitive desires?

Therefore, acceptance of the gospel could never be a completely easy or simple matter. Questionings were bound to break through. The disciples had believed that the Divine had come into their world in Jesus; that the Unseen is what Jesus said he is, "My Father and your Father"; and that the love of the Father and the grace of Jesus Christ can enter into men's hearts through the Holy Spirit. But were these convictions something more than projections of human longings and perhaps unfounded human hopes? Does God in his inmost Being correspond to the intuitions men believe they have of him? That is what the theologians of the Church necessarily were moved to ask. Even when their thinking grew intricate and difficult, what they were trying to do was to discover a path of understanding by which men might find their way home to the heart of the Reality in which our lives are held.

So there were the explorations of thought and the increasing efforts to express the faith in creeds which we have traced.

And so at length appeared the specific doctrine of the Trinity.

Tertullian, late in the second century, was the first who used the word. The Nicene Creed, in its triple affirmation, expresses the threefoldness in which God had been apprehended. But in the following years of the fourth century, men pressed on to more ultimate formulations. They were trying to find a conceptual framework within which the intellect could hold the experienced fact of one God manifested in three ways. And in the creed, probably of the fifth century, which is called the Athanasian Creed—though Athanasius himself could not have written it—here is the point to which the Church's thought had come.

This is the Catholic Faith: That we worship one God in trinity, and trinity in unity; neither confounding the persons; nor dividing the Substance. . . .

In this Trinity none is before or after another: none is greater or less than another. But the whole three Persons are co-eternal together, and co-equal.

Once this proclamation concerning the Trinity—and the Church's faith as related to it—had been put forth, it would have its unending echoes. Innumerable theologians have expounded it. Synods and assemblies of many Christian communions have reaffirmed it. In varying words but in similar substance they have said what is said in the first of the Articles of Religion in the Book of Common Prayer:

There is but one living and true God, everlasting, without body, parts, or passions; of infinite power, wisdom, and goodness; the Maker, and Preserver of all things both visible and invisible. And in unity of this Godhead there be three Persons, of one substance, power, and eternity; the Father, the Son, and the Holy Ghost.

In the doctrine of the Trinity, even when thus stated in formidable language, the central fact was and is that in it a profound religious conviction has been seeking articulate expression. Generations of Christians had known the actual influences which had come to them out of the fullness of God. Then the doctrine of the Trinity was fashioned to be as a lamp that would hold and transmit the living flame. How sufficient or insufficient that lamp may be is a matter still to be considered, but always there must be remembered the deep and glowing religious intuition which sought expression in it. "The doctrine of the Trinity in Unity of God," wrote Albert Mansbridge, "meets the needs of human nature—God above, God incarnate, God inspiring." [2] In his introductory essay to the third volume in the first series of *Nicene and Post-Nicene Fathers*, William G. T. Shedd put the conviction of many into these glowing words:

Take out of the Christian consciousness the thoughts and affections that relate to the Father, the Son, and the Holy Spirit, and there is no Christian consciousness left. The Trinity is the constitutive idea of the evangelical theology, and the formative idea of the evangelical experience. The immensity of the doctrine makes it of necessity a mystery; but a mystery which like night enfolds in its unfathomed depths the bright stars—points of light, compared with which there is no light so keen and so glittering. Mysterious as it is, the Trinity of Divine Revelation is the doctrine that holds in it all the hope of man; for it holds within it the infinite pity of the Incarnation and the infinite mercy of the redemption.[3]

And

[2] *Trodden Road* (London: J. M. Dent, 1940), p. 224.
[3] Wm. G. T. Shedd, "Introduction," *Nicene and Post-Nicene Fathers*, Vol. III. (Grand Rapids, Mich.: Wm. B. Eerdmans Co., 1956.)

116

Has not John Calvin himself asserted, in the first book of his *Institutes*, that unless we think of the unity of God as trinitarian we have no true knowledge of God at all, only the word "God" flutters through our brain, naked and void of meaning? [4]

To enter into the purposed meaning of the doctrine it is important to consider first the way in which the men who formed it thought. The early Church Fathers, in their Greco-Roman world, made use of the symbols and analogies which had particular suggestion for themselves and for their contemporaries. In the doctrine of the Trinity, they confessed God as in three Persons. When the word "person" carries the meaning which it does for present thought, then there may ensue what to modern minds—as we shall recognize presently—may seem the inexplicable problem of conceiving three Persons in God who is also One; for to us a person means a distinct psychological entity, existing within the limits of its own consciousness, and always an essentially separate self. But men who were steeped in Hellenic thought and were within the familiar associations of the Hellenic world could have a different picture in their minds when they spoke of one who was a person. In the Greek dramas an actor might wear a mask, and then another mask, as he became now one character and then another. Within that framework of thought and of expression, it was not the actor who was the *person*. The πρόσωπον, as the word was in Greek, or the *persona*, as it was in Latin, was the character whom the actor at that moment represented and whose particularity the audience thus saw enacted and heard through the lines of the play. Such was the analogy from Greek drama that shaped the thought of some of the early Fathers. The one living God was manifested

[4] Hodgson, *op. cit.*, p. 15.

in the several modes in which human hearts and minds had been aware of him.

Along with this conception drawn from the drama there was another drawn from Greek philosophy. As this came to its full development in the thought of Basil of Caesarea, Gregory of Nazianzus, and Gregory of Nyssa, late in the fourth century, a distinction was made between God's *ousia* (in Latin, his *substantia*) which meant the essential Being of God, and his *hypostases,* which were the differentiations in functioning of that essential Being. Within the Godhead were the relations of Father, Son, and Holy Spirit. In these three aspects of creator, redeemer, and inspirer, God could be separately known; yet it was the wholeness of God that was operative in each and all of these ways.

Those forms of thought were useful in the early efforts to shape a conception of the one God in his threefold manifestation which the mind could intelligibly hold. But difficulty increased with the tendency to try to pin down categorically the meaning of three Persons in the Godhead.

Sabellius, early in the third century, carried out into logical doctrine the analogy from the drama lifted up into an eternal reference: as though in the infinite reality, as suggested on the earthly stage, one Being communicated his living presence and his message through different roles in which his undivided self appeared. But the prevailing thought of his time considered that Sabellius blurred the actuality of the Incarnation and the objective presence of God in the Holy Spirit. As H. R. Mackintosh has summed up Sabellius' thought:

For him . . . the Divine in Christ has no personal subsistence, but is a mere passing phase of the one Deity, who is denoted by the name μιοπάτωρ. Three phenomenal aspects—Father, Son, and Spirit —are referred to a transcendent Godhead which remains immutable behind them all. In the *prosôpon* of the Father, God acted as Creator and Lawgiver; in the *prosôpon* of the Son as Redeemer, from the birth at Bethlehem on to the ascension; thenceforward as the Holy Spirit. Epiphanius relates that Sabellius used to compare the Father to the orb of the sun as we see it, the Son to its light, and the Spirit to its heat; while Athanasius adds that he described the Father as being *expanded* into the Son and the Spirit. . . . What is of first-rate importance in the system is Sabellius' explicit declaration that those revelational aspects of God are *successive and temporary*. For him God is not Father, Son, and Spirit simultaneously; only as one aspect ceases to be does another rise into existence. . . . On one point he stood firm—neither Son nor Spirit has personal subsistence.[5]

But though Sabellius' thought had logical consistency, it was rejected by the majority of the Church's thinkers as *modalism:* a representation of God in successive modes which failed to embody the Christian conviction that the fullness of God was given in each of the ways in which men were made aware of him. Sabellianism was accounted as a heresy; especially as Mackintosh points out, because of

its definite negation of the existence of the Divine Christ after His ascension. In His earthly life He was God; at its close He was again absorbed, like a sunbeam retracted once more to its native source in the sun. This was more than dubious Trinitarian theory: it was an attempt upon the immediate certainties of the Christian mind.[6]

As against the modalism of Sabellius, and as against *adoption-ism* and *monarchianism*, conceptions which in various degrees

[5] *Op. cit.*, p. 152.
[6] *Ibid.*, p. 153.

119

made God the Son and God the Holy Spirit derivative from and subordinate to God the Father, the Athanasian Creed declared:

> In this Trinity none is before or after another: none is greater or less than another. But the whole three Persons are co-eternal together, and co-equal. . . .
>
> For there is one person of the Father: another of the Son: and another of the Holy Ghost. But the Godhead of the Father, and of the Son, and of the Holy Ghost is all one: the glory equal, the majesty co-eternal. . . .
>
> He therefore that will be saved, must thus think of the Trinity.

It may be remembered that no less learned a person than the eminent Dr. Robert South, a seventeenth-century Englishman, was moved to exclaim, "As he that denies this fundamental article of the Christian religion may lose his soul, so he that strives to understand it may lose his wits." But alongside that whimsical exaggeration may be set the words of the German mystic, Gerhard Tersteegen: "A God understood, a God comprehended, is no God." That is to say, the greatness and glory of God cannot be caught up in any easy pattern of our thinking. It was not strange, then, that those who formulated the doctrine of the Trinity and those who afterwards held it and repeated it, should have used language that ended in paradox.

Sometimes the proclamation of the doctrine would be not so much by analysis as by unhesitant assertion, which was the way of the warm-blooded and positive Martin Luther. In his commentary on John 1:1-3, he taught:

> In the Godhead, the entire divine nature and essence passes into the Son; yet the Son, who remains in the same Godhead with the

Father, is one God together with Him. Likewise, the Holy Spirit partakes of the same divine nature with the Father and the Son. . . . This must be accepted by faith. No matter how clever, acute, and keen reason may be, it will never grasp and comprehend it. If it were susceptible to our wisdom, then God would not need to reveal it from heaven or proclaim it through Holy Scripture. So be governed by this fact and say: "I believe and confess that there is one eternal God and, at the same time, three distinct Persons, even though I cannot fathom and comprehend this. For Holy Scripture, which is God's Word, says so; and I abide by what it states.[6]

With John Calvin, in his *Institutes of the Christian Religion*, the setting forth of the doctrine is more calmly reasoned:

I am exceeding pleased with this observation of Gregory Nazianzen. I cannot think of the *One,* but I am immediately surrounded with the splendour of the *Three,* nor can I clearly discover the *Three,* but I am carried back to the *One.* Wherefore let us not imagine such a trinity of Persons, as includes an idea of separation, or does not immediately recall us to the unity. The names of Father, Son and Spirit, certainly imply a real distinction; let no one suppose them to be mere epithets, by which God is variously designated from his works; but it is a distinction, not a division.[7]

Similar to the thought of Calvin are the contemporary words of Edwin Lewis:

That a philosophical approach to God yields the concept of the Absolute may be true enough. But there is also such a thing as a religious approach to God. It may even be that the religious approach, just because it necessarily calls for a modification of the absolutist concept, is the more justifiable approach, since it takes

---

[6] *Luther's Works* (St. Louis: Concordia Publishing House, 1957), XXII, 6.
[7] Ch. 13:17.

account of a wider interpretation of facts and experiences than does the philosophical. . . . The very fact of creation presupposes an activity on the part of God. This activity reveals God. But the activity is not simple: it is multiform. Its range is very wide, and it includes the fact of Jesus Christ. Certainly God must be conceived as a Being in whose nature are those intrinsic capacities of which his diverse activities are so many expressions. The least that this yields to reflective thought is a God whose inner life is a unity of unimaginably rich diversity. The outward creativity rests back upon and manifests the inner diversity.[8]

So, for Christian faith and for those who have expounded it, there has always been the conviction of the oneness of God, and yet of the threefoldness of his manifestation. These two truths must belong together in the ultimate Reality. It was this double fact which the great Christian thinkers—whether successfully or not—were trying to express. They wanted to anchor the experience of Christian life in a conception of the nature of God that would validate the utmost they had believed. And, in the words of William Adams Brown,

It is this sense of unseen reality which gives the doctrine of the ontological Trinity its practical value. . . . Trinitarians have been unwilling to stop with a Trinity of manifestation, because this method has seemed to them to resolve the doctrine into a mere analysis of human experience. Beyond all that was human and finite they have sought to press into the immediate presence of God, that they might find their rest and peace in him.[9]

[8] *Interpretation*, Vol. XII, No. 4, p. 455. By permission of *Interpretation*.
[9] *Christian Theology in Outline* (New York: Charles Scribner's Sons, 1906), p. 161.

XI

DIFFICULTIES IN THE DOCTRINE

YET THE ATTEMPT TO EXPLICATE A DOCTRINE OF THE TRINITY has always moved on a dangerous edge. There was the constant and right desire to build a bridge of religious understanding between the felt realities and the ineffable mystery of God as he is in himself. But some of the projected bridges have been too unsubstantial for the mind to cross.

Certainly it has to be admitted that there are many people inside the churches, as well as outside, who are baffled. Hodgson himself has asked:

How many Christians today, when trying to speak of the faith by which they live, would select the doctrine of the Trinity as that to whose truth their whole being vibrates? How many laymen would not rather regard it as an unintelligible metaphysical doctrine which orthodoxy requires them to profess, but which has no direct relevance to their life or their prayers? How many clergy, as Trinity Sunday draws near, groan within themselves at the thought that it will be their duty to try to expound this dry and abstract doctrine to congregations for whom they anticipate that it will have but little interest? [1]

The chief difficulty with the doctrine, of course, is in its own

[1] *Op. cit.*, p. 177.

essential nature, for it involves the necessity of somehow bringing together two conceptions which on the face of them seem irreconcilable. On the one hand, there is the sovereign strength of Judaeo-Christian monotheism. No heir to the developed faith and awed worship which have been handed on from the Old Testament to the New could count it other than blasphemy to doubt the oneness of God.

There must be no shadow of suggestion of a multiplicity of gods, such as in the myths of the gods on Olympus, or in some other pagan pantheon. But on the other hand, there was the rich fact of religious experience. The Reality of God had come to men and women in the Christian fellowship in a threefold way. They had known the redemptive nearness of God in Jesus; they had been lifted to a new conviction of the glory and goodness of the Father because of Jesus; and because of Jesus crucified, but to their awareness also risen and exalted, there had come to them a quickened life in which they recognized the sanctifying Spirit. They must put these actualities into the framework of a unifying truth.

Yet there they confronted—and we confront—the metaphysical problem of how there can be Three in One, and yet One in Thee. It poses for the mind a task that certainly stretches whatever may be its powers of reasoning to their farthest limit. On so vast a theme all language must be tentative. Concerning the imagined inner nature of the Trinity, Augustine was right in his confession that "We say three persons, not that we wish to say it, but that we may not be reduced to silence." But even the great Augustine used analogies and illustrations which fail to say what is helpful because they attempt to say too much, as though our little invented parallels could fathom the unfathomableness of God. For example, he likens the relationship *augustine*

of the three Persons in the Oneness of the Godhead to the root, the trunk and the branches of a tree. "So . . . the root is wood, and the trunk is wood, and the branches are wood, while nevertheless it is not three woods that are thus spoken of but only one." [2] And, again, he likens the Trinity to a river, a fountain, and the draught of water drawn from the fountain. "If three cups be filled out of one fountain they may certainly be called three cups, but cannot be spoken of as three waters, but only as one all together. Yet . . . in each of them by itself there is water." From which he concludes—but who shall say convincingly?—that "in this way no one may wonder and think it absurd that we should call the Father God, the Son God, the Holy Spirit God, and that nevertheless we should say that there are not three Gods in that Trinity, but one God and one substance." [3]

In other aspects of his thinking Augustine interprets the nature of God according to the nature of the human mind. In the mind, he said, there is also the mind's love of itself and its knowledge of itself. There are memory, understanding, and will. There is also the threefold association of sight, the object seen, and the attention of the mind to what it sees. By such attempted parallelisms he sought to indicate how God can be at once the Father, Son, and Holy Spirit.

Yet it is obvious that to the religious longing for something solid on which to base its faith, this will seem a spectral sort of reasoning. What does it mean—and what would it matter—to think of God the Father as analogous to memory, and Christ the Son as analogous to understanding? This area of thinking would leave deeper needs untouched. God could seem still to

[2] *On Faith and the Creed*, ch. 9:17.
[3] *Ibid.*

be the impersonal Absolute, wrapped up in his own self-con-templation.

But Augustine's thought took a profounder range. There was the Gospel testimony that God is love. The actuality of his redeeming love had been seen in the life of Jesus. So God was not the Unrelated of the philosophers. The Father loved the Son, and the Son loved the Father. What then could speculative thinkers be led to postulate concerning God's essential nature? Augustine developed the answer which others before him had suggested. For love to be real it must be responsive, and so there must have been Persons in the Godhead between whom there could be love.

Here the reverent imagination begins to wake. One remem-bers Jesus. In him the love of God had entered the human scene, experienced our human limitations, taken upon itself the consequences of human sins, and made the ultimate vicarious sacrifice of the cross. Jesus, who thus—in the fullest term which language can find to describe him—was the beloved Son, was linked in prayer and continual devotion with the Father. So one begins to conceive the truth that this relationship was not a thing of time, but of all eternity: that from everlasting to ever-lasting there has been and is a redeemingness in God. He is not and never has been the remote Absolute, but rather the God whose inmost nature it is to create souls that can be aware of him and then to lead them to himself. So within the Being of God has there been forever the communion between himself as the Self-Existent and himself as the Redeemer, which our groping words would describe as the communion of two Persons in the God-head? Here we stand at the borders of the infinite mystery, but a mystery into which the experienced fact of the Incarnation gives us what we dare believe is guiding light. For we cannot fail to believe that the saving mercy that was in Jesus is of God, and that all the pathos of humanity which the Divine love in Jesus knew speaks in the heart of God. Thus what men saw in Jesus is eternally in the Unseen, and he "who came from God and went to God" is the Son inseparable from the Father.

But Christian experience had also a third factor. Within the lives of Christians there came the new power which they called the Holy Spirit. Religiously, that Spirit was indubitable fact. Something wholly above and beyond themselves entered into men and women to give them the lift that could have come only from God. According to the Fourth Gospel, Jesus had promised, "I will not leave you desolate; I will come to you" (14:18). He had promised also that he would pray to the Father, "and he will give you another Counselor" (14:16). In effect that double promise had been fulfilled. It was as though Jesus, though no longer with them visibly, had so entered into their minds and hearts as an indwelling presence that they could say, as St. Paul did, "henceforth I live, yet not I, but Christ liveth in me."

But how should they interpret this inner Spirit? Was it the same grace which they had known in Jesus, now come back as their risen Lord who was set free from time and space? Or was it another effluence out of the fulness of God? In the New Testament the two thoughts shift and melt one into another like the colors in a kaleidoscope. Now it is the living Christ who comes back to his disciples; then it is the Holy Spirit, another entity of God, who comes to carry on and make universal that which Christ had given. By the time the doctrine of the Trinity was formulated, this latter conception had prevailed. So, when the Godhead was conceived as a unity of Persons, those Persons now were three.

Here entered the complication which has created the greatest

127

difficulty in the doctrine. It may be possible to form a conceptual framework in which the mind and the reverent imagination can think of God transcendent and God made incarnate in Jesus as two realities in the Divine between whom there is such communion that one can dare to speak of love within the Godhead. Our human language, even at its highest, can give us only imperfect symbols; but there is something at least conceivable in a relationship between the one whom we call the Father and the one whom we call the Son. In such conception there is enough concreteness of suggestion for the word Persons to come closer to our grasp. But when the Holy Spirit is introduced as a third entity, imagination fails. According to Augustine, the three Persons in the Trinity, are "One who loves Him who is from Himself; and One who loves Him from whom He is; and Love itself." [4] But if the Holy Spirit "is love itself," or the uniting bond between the Father and the Son, as Augustine held him to be, then it is obvious that if one of three in the Trinity is only a *relationship,* the representation of three *Persons* has dissolved into a mist.

Certainly the reality of God is greater than any of our would-be interpretations of it, and certainly there can be a Trinity irrespective of what we say or do not say about it. But it is also true that we need to scrutinize our thinking and admit that even the greatest efforts of the Church to seek the truth do not always find an open road. The doctrine of the Trinity, as we have recognized, is like a lantern by which men have tried to find their way to God. So it must be held in reverent hands, lest, if it were rudely treated, the flame of its religious meaning might be lost. Yet always there is the inescapable question as to whether

[4] *On the Trinity,* Bk. VI, ch. 5:7.

the doctrine as it has been shaped is a formulation that can be fully satisfying. Was the lamp so fashioned that it does throw light; or is some of the light it is supposed to give refracted and full of shadows?

In regard to the doctrine of the Holy Spirit as a third Person in the one God, it must be admitted that the average run of would-be Christians are not illumined. I can never forget the idea which came to me as a small boy in Sunday school, and which yet lurks in the corner of my mind and moves out like an urchin of subconsciousness to pluck at the sleeve of more mature conceptions. As my teacher spoke of God the Father, God the Son, and God the Holy Spirit, I tried to picture what she meant. I saw God the Father, noble and beneficent; and Jesus, his Son, in heaven now after his life on earth. They were having a wonderful time together, and nothing else was needed. But there was the Holy Spirit, who somehow had to be got into the picture, too. As I looked I saw Jesus tall, blond, and beautiful, and the Holy Spirit short, dark, and rather shy and awkward. He seemed to be a sort of accidental and temporary member of the family. God and Jesus did their best to be nice to him, but when they could without unkindness, they sent him off on errands and resumed their happy conversation.

A naïve and childish notion, as anyone can recognize. But all the same it points up a question which cannot easily be got rid of. Is there *any* categorical conceptualization of God-in-three-persons which can avoid the feeling that it will not do? The picture created for the small boy in Sunday school was grotesque, of course. But more sophisticated efforts to represent the Trinity may no less fail. In one of the upper galleries of the Boston Public Library, opposite his magnificent frieze of the Old Testament prophets, John Singer Sargent has painted his representation of the Father, Son, and Holy Spirit. And how do they appear? As three identical figures on three Byzantine thrones, wrapped in one seamless robe. As a work of art it is not appealing. As an effort at theological interpretation it exemplifies that in which many other attempts to express the Trinity end—in stereotypes which baffle the imagination and leave religious feeling cold.

Cyril Richardson, in his recent book already referred to, has written:

> While it is necessary to make distinctions in the Godhead, these are of various kinds and do not lend themselves to a neat, trinitarian pattern. Different problems and distinctions are involved. Their terms cannot be treated as identical and summed up under the symbols of Father, Son, and Spirit. The historic forms of trinitarian thinking have frequently involved artificialities, partly because different issues have been confused, and partly because the terms "Father," "Son" and "Spirit" are ambiguous, and their meanings tend to overlap. . . . But it is in the "threeness" of the Trinity that the main artificiality lies, and I shall try to show that the essential meaning of the Trinity in its classical formulations is not necessarily connected with the number three.[5]

To label this "threeness" in the doctrine of the Trinity by so extreme a term as " artificiality" may well be challenged; but the honesty that asks whether or not the doctrine conveys the religious meaning that was at the heart of it will not be challenged. Even for the greatest Christian thinkers, language was—as it must always be—an imperfect instrument. Men first of all *live;* and the awarenesses of God that come in the process of living are infinitely swift and subtle. They can no more be pinned down

---

[5] *Op. cit.,* p. 13.

into static expression than one can put down on canvas the ineffable colors of the sunrise that every instant change. Language can suggest but never exactly circumscribe. If this be true in the area of human facts, how much more true it is when men shape the language of doctrines by which thought tries to project itself into the infinite mysteries of God.

This inability to explain the ultimate metaphysical being of the Holy Spirit can leave the restless intellect unsatisfied—as indeed how could it be otherwise for our finite minds? But always the vital matter is that the reality of the very God does come as Holy Spirit to human hearts and souls in a certainty that does not depend on explanation. As Ernest F. Scott has written:

The belief in the Spirit has always sprung out of an experience. . . . In times of religious awakening . . . men have felt themselves possessed with a quickening and uplifting power, which seemed to come directly out of a higher world.[6]

Henry Pitney Van Dusen, having referred to those and other words of Scott, has gone on to say:

So with respect to the regnancy of the Holy Spirit in Christian conviction. . . . Time and again, the Holy Spirit has dropped from the center of attention because it has been lost from the heart of experience; theological crystallization and controversy have preoccupied men's minds; reliance upon creed and cult, upon form and structure, has displaced expectation of new disclosures, sometimes with determinative influence and often with baneful effect upon men's conception of the Holy Spirit. Always, perhaps at long

---

[6] *The Spirit in the New Testament* (New York: George H. Doran Co., 1923), p. vi.

last, the Holy Spirit has returned, first as an experience and secondarily as a doctrine, to revive men's souls and banish their defeat and despair, and then to reanimate the dead skeletons of ecclesiastical organization and redeem the dry rot of dogma.[7]

Thus we have considered the difficulty in the doctrine of the Trinity which inheres in the nature of that doctrine itself. For those who would try to understand it there may be a less important, but more immediate, difficulty. Sometimes exponents of the doctrine fail to make contact with the uninstructed man. They start with too large assumptions, so that before they know it they have moved off to an unreachable distance; and the mind that needed close guidance is left helplessly at a stand.

Even some of the most admirable interpreters may not seem to make their beginning at the point which would be most surely understandable. They may recognize, as Leonard Hodgson has said, that "the theology has no meaning for us unless it interprets our living religion." [8] But the reader may not be conscious that where they start is where his actual religion is. The very title of a book may come to him with a grey mist of remoteness trailing round it. Both of the two recent and exceedingly suggestive books already quoted, Hodgson's and Richardson's—and others before them—are entitled *The Doctrine of the Trinity*. Each book, and especially Hodgson's, goes on to deal richly with the experienced spiritual realities out of which the doctrine could naturally develop. But the title fails to suggest at first an on-the-earth reality upon which the loftier thought may inductively be built. Instead, it suggests an assumed conclusion that there *is* a Trinity and that this prejudgment up in the philosophical

[7] *Spirit, Son and Father* (New York: Charles Scribner's Sons, 1958), pp. 27-28. By permission.
[8] *Op. cit.*, p. 176.

stratosphere will be brought down to make the facts fit into its pattern. To try deliberately to avoid that danger is the reason why the first word in the title of this particular book is *Jesus*. To start with him is to start where both thought and feeling can sense a contact which may have for everyone some real solidity.

When Christian thinkers express the doctrine of the Trinity in terms that seem to imply its authoritative finality, the persuasiveness of the doctrine is not strengthened, but weakened. Hodgson has written:

There is general agreement that the doctrine of the Trinity is a revealed doctrine. It is, for example, for St. Thomas Aquinas the classic example of the kind of doctrine which can only be made known to man by divine revelation, and Calvin's exposition of it is an exposition of what he accepts as biblical revelation. . . . The Blessed Trinity is not some incomprehensible mystery which we dimly worship from without: it is the revealed nature of the God "in whom we live and move and have our being," as well known and familiar to the Christian, and as often unnoticed, as the air he breathes.[9]

Although in what those words intend they are the expression of profound spiritual reality, in what they *say* they can be misleading. For in the sense of what the word "revealed" may convey to most readers, the doctrine of the Trinity is not a revealed doctrine. It has not come down like a document from heaven with God's imprimatur upon it, shining and complete like some golden Book of Mormon. To think of a doctrine as revealed is to fall into the error that so often has stereotyped religious belief. God is not revealed in formulated propositions or codes—not in scribal law, nor in scriptural canon regarded as infallible, nor in

[9] *Ibid.*, pp. 16, 50.

the painfully hammered-out conclusions of earnest but all-too-human ecclesiastical councils. God is the living God who is most certainly made known, not by what men say about him, but by what he does and by what he is in history and in the direct awareness of human souls.

The doctrine of the Trinity thus is not a revelation; it is a *derivation*. It is what the mind derives as its own most reverent and thoughtful interpretation of the infinite Reality which is directly known only in the actualities of life. Therefore the doctrine of the Trinity, insofar as it is true to the living revelation in the Incarnate Lord, has the authority of the road sign that says to us, "In this direction is the Way to God"; but no language or name upon the sign can presume to be a final indication of the inner nature of the infinite One to whom it points.

How difficult it is to find terms that could express the inner nature of God and represent the Trinity is evident enough when one observes how kaleidoscopic are the descriptive words that equally eminent theologians use. Vincent Taylor, in *The Person of Christ in New Testament Teaching*,[10] notes that C. Welch "proposes that we should use the term 'Person' in respect of the Triune God and 'modes of being' (or 'existence') for the distinctions within His Trinity." But Taylor's own judgment is that

It does not seem that any advantage is gained by speaking of God as "Person" rather than by using C. C. J. Webb's phrase "personality in God," or by using "modes of being" instead of "persons" for the distinctions of Father, Son and Holy Spirit within the unity of the Divine Being.[11]

[10] (London: Macmillan and Co. Ltd., 1958), p. 253.
[11] *Op. cit.*

Lionel Thornton, however, in *The Incarnate Lord* writes that

If we speak of "personality in God" at all, the phrase must be carefully guarded to avoid either Unitarian or tritheistic implications. . . . On the other hand the phrase "One Absolute Individuality," . . . asserts a theistic position without introducing inconvenient uncertainties as to the nature of personality in God. Thus the phrase *Three Persons in One Absolute Individuality* appears to strike the right balance.[12]

But George F. Thomas warns that "the danger of the Trinitarian formula, 'one Substance in three Persons,' has always been that the *eternal aspects* of the Divine activity tend to be taken as *independent centers* of consciousness and volition, as 'persons' in the modern sense of individual entities with a substantial existence of their own"; [13] and, in the words of J. S. Whale, Christian thought has "acknowledged in the Godhead, not one Individual nor three Individuals, but a personal unity existing eternally in three eternal modes or functions." [14]

So in any meditation upon what may be the reality of the Trinity there needs to be humility of assertion, but always the unwearied quest for the living truth which religious intuition reaches after. All thought and speech concerning it, wrote Lionel Thornton, "must be utterly inadequate, like the naïve chatter of children concerning the mysteries of life and the universe. Yet, if we are to be recipients of the light . . . we cannot remain silent. . . . Faith must seek to understand." [15]

[12] (London: Longmans, Green and Co., 1928), pp. 414-15.
[13] *The Christian Answer, op. cit.,* p. 113.
[14] *Christian Doctrine* (Cambridge University Press, 1941), p. 116.
[15] *Op. cit.,* p. 416.

To sum up the matter, we may listen again to the words of one who was great not only in intellect but in the intuitions of his soul, Augustine:

These things, however, can easily be spoken and believed; but *seen* so as to reveal how they are in themselves, they absolutely cannot be, except by the pure heart. . . . Neither should we make any affirmation on the subject of things unseen rashly, as if we had knowledge, but [only modestly] as believing. For these things cannot be seen except by the heart made pure.[16]

[16] *On Faith and the Creed*, ch. 9:20.

XII

SOME MODERN INTERPRETATIONS

THE EFFORT TO RECONCILE WHAT IS CERTAINLY THE DEEP—
and it may seem the irreconcilable—difference between the conception of God as One and the conception of three Persons in that
Oneness, was of course not ended in the early centuries. Thomas
Aquinas wrestled with it again, and so have other profound
thinkers of medieval and of modern times. Of two notable books
that deal with this problem of the doctrine of the Trinity which
have been published in recent years, one is Dorothy Sayers' *The
Mind of the Maker*.

In the preface to this book Dorothy Sayers wrote:

The Christian affirmation . . . is that the Trinitarian structure
which can be shown to exist in the mind of man and in all his
works is, in fact, the integral structure of the universe, and corres-
ponds, not by pictorial imagery but by a necessary uniformity of
substance, with the nature of God, in Whom all that is exists.[1]

This, as will at once be recognized, is in tune with the thought
of Augustine that "A Trinitarian structure of being is not a thing
incomprehensible or unfamiliar to you; you know of many such
within the created universe." [2] The distinctive value of her book

[1] (New York: Harcourt, Brace & Company, 1941), p. xiii. Copyright 1942,
Dorothy L. Sayers.
[2] *On the Trinity.*

is that among the many such "analogies that might imaginably be explored," she follows the one which is most vivid to her: the analogy of the mind of the creative writer—with the recognition also that *"mutatis mutandis,* what is true of the writer is true also of the painter, the musician and all workers of creative imagination in whatever form." [3]

Assuming then that in this highest functioning of the human mind there is, so to speak, the radio beam that is most surely to be followed in the reverent flight of imagination toward the infinity of God, she distinguishes in that mind three elements: the Creative Idea, the Creative Energy, and the Creative Power.

The meaning of these, in their distinctness and yet in their intricate and indissoluble relationship, is vividly portrayed in her analysis of what actually happens in the creative mind. When the writer or the artist becomes a creator, the "Idea" precedes any mental or physical work upon the materials, yet the "formulation of the Idea in the writer's mind is not the Idea itself, but its self-awareness in the Energy."

With Shakespeare, for example, when he created *Hamlet,* there was first the Idea which projected itself forward in intention to the drama, as yet nonexistent, which his mind conceived. Then the Idea had to be made concrete reality by the creative Energy which embodied it in characters, in scenes and settings, and in its whole expression within the terms of actual life. The Idea becomes explicit only when it is thus incarnated by the creative Energy, but always that Energy is governed by the reference back to the sovereign Idea.

When these two go forward in attunement of purpose, there is Power. This "Creative Power," Dorothy Sayers goes on,

---

[3] Sayers, *op. cit.,* p. 37.

is the third "Person" of the writer's Trinity. It is not the same thing as the Energy (which for greater clearness I ought perhaps to have called "the Activity"), though it proceeds from the Idea and the Energy together. It is the thing which flows back to the writer from his own activity and makes him, as it were, the reader of his own book. It is also, of course, the means by which the Activity is communicated to other readers and which produces a corresponding re-'sponse in them. In fact, from the reader's point of view, it *is* the book. By it, they perceive the book, both as a process in time and as an eternal whole, and react to it dynamically.[4]

Carrying this analogy of the creative artist into the interpretations of the Trinity, the summary is this:

The Creative Idea, passionless, timeless, beholding the whole work complete at once, the end in the beginning: . . . this is the image of the Father.

The Creative Energy (or *Activity*) begotten of that Idea, working in time from the beginning to the end, with sweat and passion, being incarnate in the bonds of matter: . . . is the image of the Word.

The Creative Power, the meaning of the work and its response in the lively soul: . . . is the image of the indwelling Spirit.

And those three are one, each equally in itself the whole work, whereof none can exist without the other: and this is the image of the Trinity.[5]

But *is* it an image of the Trinity? Full of spiritual imagination and illuminating though *The Mind of the Maker* is, it does not

[4] *Ibid.*, p. 40-41.
[5] *Ibid.*, p. 37.

successfully illuminate *that* mystery. What it does is something different. By its analysis of how in the human mind the Idea becomes creative, it throws suggestive light upon the ancient problem of how the Absolute may also be the Related, and of how that which remains transcendent can also be embodied in the immanent. It helps by its analogy to reveal how God, who is above all life, can yet enter into life. But an attempted parallelism projected from the facts of the human mind simply does not bridge the gulf between our utmost conceptions and the mystery involved in the doctrine of the Trinity. What goes on in the functioning of the mind that is all the while one individual still falls short of expressing those essential distinctions within the being of God which are represented by the concrete names of Father, Son, and Holy Spirit.

The other significant recent book is Leonard Hodgson's *The Doctrine of the Trinity*, already referred to. Hodgson, like Dorothy Sayers, and like that greater precursor, Augustine, seeks to reach a conception of the Trinity through contemplation of the human mind. As he himself indicates, his thought was sparked by the lectures delivered at Edinburgh, and the book subsequently published, by Dr. John Laird on *Problems of the Self*. It had been pointed out that

the human self is known to us in the three activities of thinking, feeling and willing. Each of these is only known to us in its active exercise, when it is always concerned with some object which gives it content. Each of these activities is distinct from the other two: thinking is a distinct activity, not to be identified or confused with feeling or willing, and each of the others is equally distinct. Yet they interpermeate one another in such a way that in human life no one exists except as conditioned by the others.[6]

[6] Hodgson, *op. cit.*, pp. 85-86.

What then, asks Hodgson, is the principle that makes these three aspects in the life of a human being unified and continuous? There is no discernible entity of the self *other* than these three activities. No one of them, neither thinking, nor willing, nor feeling, can be said to be more central than the remaining two. Therefore "we are left with a mysterious unity in trinity, a unity which is an object of faith postulated by our reason in order to account for the observed trinity of activities." [7]

Then Hodgson goes on to consider what is the nature of this unity between the several functionings of the human being, and by inference what may be the unity that in God binds three Persons into Oneness. There is a unity, he says, which is *arithmetical* and the criterion of which is the absence of multiplicity. The creature which most nearly exemplifies the bare arithmetical unity is the unicellular amoeba. But there is also an *organic* unity; and the higher we go in the scale of life, the greater the complexity of this organic unity becomes. The simpler type of unity is easier to grasp, but this does not mean that it is more real. On the contrary, the highest type of unity is reached not by decreasing the number or variety of the elements within it, but by the heightening of a unifying power within which a multiplicity of functions operate as a living whole.

Therefore, Hodgson reasons, the divine unity can be a dynamic unity actively unifying in one divine life the lives of the three divine Persons. With our imperfectly integrated selves, this complete organic unity is beyond our full comprehension. But, for Hodgson's thought:

The essence of our faith is that there is in the Godhead the perfect instance of this kind of unity of which we have imperfect analogues

[7] *Ibid.*, p. 87.

on earth. When we have learned to measure by a scale of intensity of unifying power we no longer think that because the elements in the Godhead are not sub-personal activities, but complete persons, the degree of unity must be less than in the human self and that consequently the doctrine is tritheistic. Seeing that the degree of unification demanded so far exceeds anything within our experience, how mysterious, tremendous and fascinating, we argue, must be the intensity of that unifying power which constitutes the unity of the Blessed Trinity.[8]

But the trouble with Hodgson's thought, fresh and vigorous though it be, is that if his reasoning were followed fully it would prove too much. Not only is there danger, as Gustaf Aulen has noted, that Hodgson's thought may come close to tritheism; there is the further question as to why his conception of the Persons in the Trinity should stop short at three. Does the parallelism with Godhead drawn from the constitution of the human mind start with a premise which is itself delimited and therefore artificial? Augustine assumed the human mind to be made up of memory, understanding, and will; Hodgson, following John Laird, uses the more familiar terms: thinking, feeling, and willing.

In each case the assumed threeness makes the convenient pattern for interpreting a heavenly Trinity. But, as Cyril Richardson has acutely asked, what of other elements in the mind that might equally well be counted? What of the imagination? And if there are conscious relations, what of the unconscious ground?

The fact of the matter is, an analysis of inner relations can be posed in an indefinite number of terms. There is no necessity about

[8] *Ibid.*, p. 96.

142

the number three . . . . Once . . . the magic spell of unity is broken, we are inevitably driven to an indefinite number. If society is our analogy with the Godhead, then the more members there are, the more love abounds.[9]

A still more recent evidence of the endless fascination which the mystery of the Trinity holds for human thinking is Henry P. Van Dusen's *Spirit, Son and Father*. Reaching out—as the inquiring mind will always do—for a conception of the Trinity which can more nearly be brought within the framework of our understanding, he uses "the analogy of an individual human person in three aspects of his self-expression, in three functions and sets of relationships." The person from whom his analogy is developed is Theodore Roosevelt, in "at least three ways in which [he] could be, and was in fact, known by his contemporaries." In the first place, there was Theodore Roosevelt, the public figure, politician, statesman, and president of the United States, portrayed in his *Autobiography*. Second, there was the warm-blooded, virile man-among-men, hunter, explorer, leader of his Rough Riders, seen most clearly in his *Winning of the West*. And then there was the rollicking, delightsome playmate with boys and girls in the home at Sagamore Hill, revealed in his *Letters to His Children*.

"Which was the true Theodore Roosevelt?" Van Dusen asks.

One might have thought he knew well one of these "persons" and never suspected that there was another, two others. The three avenues of acquaintances lead to three different Theodore Roosevelts; no, not "three persons," but one person in three separate "modes of operation."

If this can be true of almost any finite person—and a hundred

[9] Cyril Richardson, *op. cit.*, p. 112.

143

others might be substituted—how much more of the Infinite Person, the Living God.[10]

That could be said to sound like Sabellianism, albeit very attractive Sabellianism and kindling to the imagination. But whatever name in the vocabulary of theological tradition be given to it, the analogy of the three "modes of operation" in Theodore Roosevelt is plainly different from the thought of Hodgson that "the elements in the Godhead are not subpersonal activities, but complete persons." Again there is illustrated the fact that any attempted description of the inner being of the Trinity can, at best, only be an inadequate projection of that threefold awareness of God which Christian experience feels and by which it is possessed.

Perhaps there is something in the structure of the human mind that inclines it instinctively to think in terms of threeness when it is reaching toward what may seem to it the synthesis of truth. J. A. MacCulloch has pointed out how often this appears in the religious conceptions of mankind. In the Babylonian tradition "there is the triad of the god Merodach, his consort Zarpanitu, and their son Nebo, the revealer of his father's will." [11] In Indian religion there are Brahma, Shiva, and Vishnu. "Most Buddhist works begin with an invocation to Buddha, Dharma and Sangha, viz. the three Holy or Precious Ones of Buddhism." [12] And for Egypt there was the divine family of Osiris, Isis, and Horus.

If the process of thought that led to the formulation of the doctrine of the Trinity may thus seem to reflect a tendency

[10] *Op. cit.*, p. 174.
[11] *Comparative Theology* (London: Methuen & Co., 1903), p. 88.
[12] *Ibid.*, p. 95.

which has also been operative in other religious concepts, there yet appears a profound difference when one perceives the basis on which the specific Christian conviction rests. As William Fulton of the University of Aberdeen has expressed it:

What lends a special character to the Christian doctrine of the Trinity is its close association with the distinctive Christian view of divine incarnation. In other religions and religious philosophies we meet with the idea of divine incarnation, but it may be claimed that nowhere is the union of God and man so concrete and definite, and so universal in its import as in the Christian religion. As Augustine said, if in the books of the Platonists it was to be found that "in the beginning was the Word," it was not found there that "the Word became flesh and dwelt among us." It is the very central truth of Christianity that God was historically manifest in Christ. . . . This Christian faith in the incarnation of the Divine Word (λογος [logos], sermo, ratio) in the man Christ Jesus, with whom the believer is united through the fellowship of the Holy Spirit, constitutes the distinctive basis of the Christian doctrine of the Trinity.[13]

Yet even in Christianity the conception of the Trinity may have its sovereign meaning blurred. It is curious to observe what Roman Catholic cultus has gradually done. It has either added another figure to what had previously been the Trinity, or it has effected a substitution. The so-called veneration, but in actual practice the worship, of the Virgin has exalted her to a position in the Godhead. As "The Queen of Heaven" and as intercessor, she has overshadowed the Holy Spirit. Here is virtually a new Trinity, and one which has powerful appeal to the untutored emotions. It embodies the instinct, old as primi-

[13] Article on the Trinity in *Encyclopaedia of Religion and Ethics* (New York: Charles Scribner's Sons, 1925), XII, 458. Used by permission.

tive religion, to seek a mother-figure, and to have a goddess as well as God. Such worship, wholly unscriptural, is, as Frederick W. Robertson expressed it,

an idolatry: in modern Romanism a pernicious and most defiling one. The worship of Mary overshadows the worship of the Son. The love given her is so much taken from Him. Nevertheless let us not hide from ourselves the eternal truth of the idea which lies beneath the temporary falsehood of the dogma. Overthrow the idolatry; but do it by substituting the truth.[14]

For what does the cult of the Virgin illustrate but this—that the emotions will reach out in an invented direction when the real meaning of Christian redemption does not burn through formulas and reach the heart. The doctrine of the Trinity is the unresting effort of human thought to express the truth that does most surely satisfy the heart, and that only in ignorance will be sought through Mary or any other lesser intermediary— the truth that the Saving Love was manifested on earth in Jesus, and that it is what was seen in Jesus that is the Reality of the eternal God and that can come as the transforming Spirit into our own souls.

It is possible for this living truth to be obscured when any attempted explanation of the Trinity is made into a rigid proposition. Every would-be statement of the doctrine must be held, not as a dogma, but as a directive. The end is in line with the beginning, which is Jesus; and interpretations of the Trinity succeed or fail according to the measure in which they do or do not transmit the central flame of Christian faith—that "through him we have access in one Spirit to the Father."

---

[14] *Sermons on Bible Subjects* (New York: E. P. Dutton & Co.,), p. 224.

XIII

WHEN THE
DOCTRINE ENDS IN DEDICATION

How shall we bring now to some final synthesis the lines of thought which have been followed? And what can the Trinity mean to us for our minds and for our souls?

The essential answer must be double: for our minds, never a final formulation; for our souls, the communication of living power from a Reality that can be experienced, no matter how far the would-be explorations of the intellect fall short.

"Never a final formulation." To admit that is not to be lacking in respect for the great succession of Christian thinkers, for Church councils, and for all in every generation who have meditated on God. It is only to recognize the profundity of those realms of thought into which they tried reverently to carry the lamps of their partial perceptions. The truest thinking about the ineffable wonder of God has always been, and must always be, that which is most humble and most tentative. As John Robinson said to the departing pilgrims, "The Lord has more truth yet to break forth from His Holy Word." Doctrines of the Trinity may become stultifying whenever they presume to say, "This is it." The utmost that can ever be said is, "This may suggest it. This is a road sign put up to point in the direction in which the experience of life has seemed to lead."

147

Symbols change their value as time goes on. Terms that once seemed best to represent the felt truth may need to be reconsidered—even the central term itself. As William Newton Clarke has written in *The Christian Doctrine of God*, "That which was adopted in the fifth century was not a Doctrine of Trinity, but of Triunity." And he continued:

It was not merely the existence of the eternal Three that was affirmed: it was affirmed that the Three eternally constituted the unity of God. In the one God there existed Father, Son, and Spirit, which three were declared necessary to the making up of that unity wherein God is forever perfect. It is plain that in such a doctrine the element of unity was as essential as that of Trinity: indeed it was the element of unity alone that gave it standing as a Christian doctrine. Trinity without unity would have been explicit tritheism, which would have been polytheism; and by no possibility could plain tritheism have been admitted among the ideas of Christianity. As a matter of fact, the historic doctrine absolutely repudiated all charges of tritheism, and made the strongest affirmation of the unity of the God in whom Trinity inhered. How much truer to fact it would have been if the accepted doctrine had been called the doctrine of Triunity, and how many misunderstandings and confusions might thus have been avoided! One practical testimony to the propriety of such nomenclature is at hand. Agelong though the use of the word Trinity has been, no one has ever ventured to be so consistent in the use of terms as to speak of the trine God. But the adoration of the Triune God has been perpetual.[1]

And if there is a danger of "misunderstandings and confusions" in the word Trinity, much more may there be in the adjective *trinitarian*, when that is made into a cast iron framework outside the literal definition of which there must be considered to be

[1] (New York: Charles Scribner's Sons, 1909), p. 233. By permission.

148

no orthodox faith. In the word there is the reflection of precious values, but it is misused when it is made part of a harsh antithesis. In its fullness, Christian faith is not only trinitarian but also unitarian. The oneness of God is an article of belief that must never be obscured by the kind of metaphysical analysis that can leave the mind of the would-be Christian so baffled as to despair of finding God intelligible at all.

There is a sort of trinitarianism which in some of its dogmatic expressions can have that effect. In the long history of Christian thinking there have been those who in their intense desire to represent the richness of God's manifestation have used such overemphasis in language as to make it seem as though there were three gods. They have represented the three Persons of the Godhead

as consulting together, sometimes in "the council-chamber of the Trinity," as making mutual covenants among themselves, and as exerting influence upon one another, in ways that necessarily implied separate wills and sometimes involved differences in character.[2]

The result has been that some honest minds in every generation, assuming that these descriptions represented orthodoxy, have supposed that there was no place in orthodox Christianity for them.

But what ought trinitarian faith essentially to mean, and what is the touchstone of its truth? Not any single formulation, but the living conviction which it has sought—always imperfectly and by partial symbols—to express. This conviction is that there is a threefold experience for Christian souls, and that this threefold experience finds its unity in God.

[2] *Ibid.*, p. 234.

It is in the light of this experience that the conception of the Trinity stands out in living power. "Why have Christians always felt," asks George F. Thomas, "that, difficult as it is to conceive, the Trinitarian view of God has a profundity that is lacking in the abstract monotheism of Judaism and Mohammedanism?" And he goes on to answer:

The reason is that the activity of God as Creator and Ruler of the world appears different from His activity as Redeemer of mankind in Christ and that both appear different from His activity as the indwelling Spirit which inspires the lives of those who put their trust in Him. The doctrine of the Trinity is an assertion of the reality of these ways in which God shows Himself to Christians, and an insistence upon the source of them in the eternal being of God. Historically, it arose out of the conviction of Christians that in Christ the divine had decisively entered into human life and that the process of redemption thus begun had been continued in the lives of his followers by the Holy Spirit of God. It meant that God was truly and fully revealed both in Christ and in the Spirit, that no mere *temporary modes* but *eternal aspects of the Divine Being* were manifested in them. Philosophically, the doctrine has also served to free Christians from the tendency of abstract monotheism to picture God as simple and undifferentiated unity utterly separated from the rich diversity of the world. It symbolizes the diversity within unity of God: His transcendent Sovereignty, redemptive Love, and indwelling spiritual Presence.[3]

God's "transcendent Sovereignty" has been acknowledged in other religions and in other ways. But God experienced as "redemptive Love, and indwelling spiritual Presence" has come to human souls most surely as they have drawn close in thought and imagination to the Incarnate Lord. It could be imagined, of

[3] *The Christian Answer, op. cit.,* p. 113.

course, that realization of God as redemptive love and a corresponding sense of his indwelling presence might have come to men if there had been no Jesus to dwell among them as the living Word. But the actual fact is that through Jesus, and only through him, has that realization been lifted to its supreme warmth and vividness. It was because men had seen Jesus that they and their successors could make the tremendous declaration that "In this the love of God was made manifest, that God sent his only Son into the world, so that we might live through him." And to live through him means life made subject to the purpose that controlled *his* life. He was seen to be God's Son because in him the love of God was burning. He was God's Son because he had come as the infinite compassion which goes to the rescue of the neediest of the Father's children. When *you* are moved to do that, he was saying to those who listened to his parable of the Judgment, then you are on the road to finding the presence of God; and if you refuse, then you go out into the dark. "As you did it, or did it not, to one of the least of these my brethren, you did it, or did it not, to me."

It is possible for men to reach up toward God without being conscious much of Christ or wanting to have him reflected in what could be the Holy Spirit in their hearts—possible thus to have no ground of specific desire out of which the meaning of the Trinity can grow. The question then will be not whether they have a religion or no religion, but whether the religion that they have will possess the richness which belongs to the Christian faith in its full heritage.

Religion can be narrowed to a single emphasis. There is a religion which is man's response to the awesomeness of the universe, and his submission to a will that is beyond his knowing. Then the Almighty, in the words of Job, is

> he who removes mountains, and they know it not,
> when he overturns them in his anger;
> who shakes the earth out of its place,
> and its pillars tremble. . . .
> Lo, these are but the outskirts of his ways,
> and how small a whisper do we hear of him!
> But the thunder of his power who can understand?
>
> —Job 9:56; 26:14

Thus religion may be a hushed reverence before the Infinite, which is to be accepted and obeyed as the Moslem accepts the will of Allah, or as the Stoic accepts the universal law to which all life must submit. So the greatness of God is recognized; but it is not a God whom the emotions of the heart feel near.

Again religion may be held to mean the experience of the mystic. Then God does seem to be apprehended in a direct communion. But mysticism may dissolve in subjective vagueness. There is a consciousness of God; but God as a directing purpose, and as the objective revelation of what active life and service ought to be, is still unrealized.

But suppose there is another experience by which the other two become illumined. Suppose that in our world the nature of God has been made manifest in a human life. Then there must grow—as there has grown—the great threefold assurance that is the Christian faith. In Jesus whom the disciples knew, in Jesus who comes alive again for those who seek him in the Gospels, men have encountered an ultimate judgment and at the same time a redeeming love which have made their deepest intuition say: *this* is the reality of God. Because of Jesus they have believed that the Infinite in whom our lives are held is no uncaring fate, but the Father whom Jesus trusted. And those stirrings of desired goodness within us, which at their best are too

152

high to be our own creation and are felt as the promptings of a Holy Spirit, become most dynamic and definite when they are shaped in the pattern of Jesus. In this triunity of fact is the oneness of God.

Thus, if it is vitally understood, the word trinitarian can be the banner of a great spiritual loyalty. But the word, because of the dust of linguistic controversies, can be ambiguous; and the ultimate name for the saving faith is neither unitarian nor trinitarian. It is *Christ*-ian. When that faith has been most glowing, it has always been because its heartbeat was in the centrality of Christ. It was what men had experienced in Jesus that made them look with new trust and confidence to the Eternal One as being "The God and Father of our Lord Jesus Christ." In the ministry of Jesus, which came to its awful climax on the cross, they saw the meaning of redemption; and it was the criterion which they had in him that controlled the meaning of life in the Spirit and kept it from turning into emotional vagaries.

The direct reality of the risen Lord was what the Christian creeds—even in their seemingly most abstruse terms, as in those of the Council of Chalcedon—were trying to express; and that direct reality is what can come again to living souls. Phillips Brooks, great man and one of the greatest interpreters of Christian truth in modern times, not long before his sudden and early death was asked by a young clergyman to tell the secret of his life. He was not given to speaking easily of his own inner experiences, but deeply moved by this request, he answered:

I am sure you will not think that I dream that I have any secret to tell. I have only the testimony to bear which any friend may fully bear to his friend when he is cordially asked for it, as you have asked me.

Indeed the more I have thought it over, the less in some sense I have seemed to have to say. And yet the more sure it has seemed to me that these last years have had a peace and fulness which there did not use to be. I say it in deep reverence and humility. I do not think it is the mere quietness of advancing age. I am sure it is not indifference to anything which I used to care for. I am sure that it is a deeper knowledge and truer love of Christ. . . .

I cannot tell you how personal this grows to me. He is here. He knows me and I know Him. It is no figure of speech. It is the reallest thing in the world. And every day makes it realler. And one wonders with delight what it will grow to as the years go on.[4]

Such was and is the reality out of which the doctrine of the Trinity has grown. Always the reality is greater than the expression of it; and that needs to be continually remembered, so that rigid formulas may not be substituted for the living faith. If trinitarianism overweeningly assumes that it can ever be more than an effort in fallible words to interpret God through Christ, it can become a cramping dogmatism. But when unitarianism abandons—as it almost fatally tends to do—the centrality of Christ and turns toward a miscellaneous eclecticism,[5] then it has lost the distinctive power that has belonged to the Church only when it has proclaimed, "Jesus Christ is Lord."

So the theme with which this book began comes to its conclusion. The doctrine of the Trinity, whenever it carries the

[4] Alexander V. G. Allen, *Life and Letters of Phillips Brooks* (New York: E. P. Dutton & Co., 1901), III, 454-455.

[5] Note the recent insistence of many Unitarians that their church should no longer be labeled as specifically Christian, but regarded as expressing a sort of universal religiousness; and the recent dropping of the word Christian from the title of the most important Unitarian journal, which since 1821 had been *The Christian Register.*

fragrance and the fruitfulness of a living truth, is rooted in the remembrance of the Word made flesh. It was what they saw and felt in the Master whom they loved and followed that made the disciples aware of God; and when they had seemed to lose him on the dreadful day of crucifixion and then his living presence came back to them in his risen power, they knew through him the greatness of God that was beyond all words to express: God touching them in him, God in his eternity interpreted through him, God in the Spirit that brought him home to their hearts.

From that same prompting the great belief and the saving experience can always come. In St. Patrick's hymn one of the verses begins,

> I bind this day to me for ever,
> By power of faith, Christ's Incarnation.

Only when that is true does it most surely follow, that

> I bind unto myself to-day
> The power of God to hold and lead.

INDEX

Abraham, 73

Acts, Holy Spirit in book of, 57-58

Adoptionism, 119

Allen, Alexander V. G., *The Continuity of Christian Thought*, 74

Amos, 17

Apocalyptic concept of Messiah, 20, 24

Apostles' Creed, 41, 79

Aquinas, Thomas, 133, 137

Arianism, 85

Arians, 83, 84

Arius, 82, 99

Arnold, Matthew, 18

Athanasian Creed, 115, 120

Athanasius, 83-84, 85, 86, 99, 115

Augustine, 124-25, 126, 136, 137, 140, 142, 145

Aulen, Gustaf, 142

Babylonian religion, 144

Baillie, Donald, *God Was in Christ*, 93

Barry, F. R., *The Relevance of Christianity*, 90

Barth, Karl, 87, 100, 101, 102, 105

Basil of Caesarea, 118

Basilides, 75, 76

Bencosiba, 19

Book of Common Prayer, 15, 115

Brahma, 144

Brooks, Phillips, 153-54

Brown, William Adams, *Christian Theology in Outline*, 122

Browning, Robert, *A Death in the Desert*, 43, 46

Brunner, Emil, 100, 101-2, 103 n.

Buchan, John, *Mountain Meadow*, 101

Buddha, 90, 144

Buddhism, 144

Caird, J., *Fundamental Ideas*, 104

Calvin, John, 117, 121, 133

Cappadocian fathers, 95

Cephas, 36

Chalcedon, Council of, 15, 79, 92

Chalmers, James, "The Expulsive Power of a New Affection," 31

Christ. *See* Jesus

Christian Register, The, 154 n.

Church fathers, 117

Circumcision, 73

Circumincessio, 95

Clarke, William Newton, *The Christian Doctrine of God*, 148, 149

Clement of Alexandria, 79, 89-90

Coffin, Henry Sloane, 97

Constantine, 81

Constantinople, Council of, 15

Conversion, William James on, 33

Corinthian church, 59

Cornelius, 58

Crucifixion, 22

Cruden, Alexander, *A Complete Concordance to the Old and New Testament*, 52

Daniel, 20, 49
Dead Sea Scrolls, 44
Demiurge, 76, 77
Deutero-Isaiah, 55
Dharma, 144
Dionysius, bishop of Alexandria, 82

Easton, Burton S., 88
Ebionites, 73
Egyptian religion, 144
Elijah, 17
Eternal Road, The, 47
Ezekiel, 55

Fairbairn, A. M., *The Place of Christ in Modern Theology*, 84
Fisher, George Park, *History of Christian Doctrine*, 75, 76
Fourth Gospel, 14, 43-51, 73
 Holy Spirit in, 65-67, 127
 Incarnation in, 69, 71
 interpretation of Jesus, 45
 origin, 43-44
 purpose, 44
 source of its influences, 49
Francis of Assisi, 111
Frank, Glenn, 112
Fulton, William, 145

Gadara, wild man of, 30
Gideon, 54
Gnosticism, 47, 74-78, 83, 85, 99
Gnostics, 79
God
 conceived as three persons, 117-18
 Hebrew concept of, 17, 53
 inmost nature of, 82-96, 97-98
 Platonic thought concerning, 99
Greek drama, 117

Greek philosophy, 118
Gregory of Nazianzus, 118
Gregory of Nyssa, 118
Grenfell, Wilfred, 111

Hadrian, 19
Hamlet, 138
Hardy, Thomas, "God's Funeral," 108-9
Henley, William Ernest, "Invictus," 112
Hodgson, Leonard, *The Doctrine of the Trinity*, 16, 105, 123, 132, 133, 140, 141-42, 144
Holy Spirit, 52-67, 127, 128, 129, 131
 in Acts, 57-58
 as creative power, 53-54
 in Fourth Gospel, 65-67
 in Old Testament, 53-55
 in Paul's letters, 60-64
 in Synoptic Gospels, 55-57
Horus, 144
Hosea, 17

Incarnation, 69-80, 82-96, 97, 99, 100, 104, 106, 107, 145, 155
Indian religion, 144
Inge, Dean, *Science and Ultimate Truth*, 113
Irenaeus, 79
Isaiah, 17, 26; *see also* Deutero-Isaiah
Isis, 144
Israel, 17
 concept of God, 53, 69, 97
 expectation of Messiah, 18-20, 26-27

James, 21
James, William, *The Varieties of Religious Experience*, 30, 33
Jeremiah, 90
Jerome, 73

Jesus
  his humanness, 48
  proof of his greatness, 18
  as Son of God, 69-72
  as Son of man, 49
  as Word of God, 49-50, 65, 74, 145
Job, 109, 152-53
John, 21, 43, 78
John, Gospel of. *See* Fourth Gospel
John, the Elder, of Ephesus, 44
Judas, 27
Judas of Galilee, 19
Justin Martyr, 74

Knox, John, 18, 39

Laird, John, *Problems of the Self*, 140, 142
Lane, Franklin K., 108
Lewis, Edwin, *Interpretation*, 121-22
Lindsay, T. M., *A History of the Reformation*, 86
Logos. *See* Word of God
Luther, Martin, 28, 120-21

MacCulloch, J. A., *Comparative Theology*, 144
McGiffert, A. C., *The God of the Early Christians*, 85
Macgregor, W. M., 33-34
Mackintosh, H. R., *The Doctrine of the Person of Jesus Christ*, 104, 118-19
MacLeish, Archibald, *J. B.*, 109
Mansbridge, Albert, *Trodden Road*, 116
Marcion, 76-77, 110
Marcus Aurelius, 74
Mary Magdalene, 22
Merodach, 144
Messiah
  Israel's expectation of, 19-20, 26-27

Messiah—*cont'd*
  and the Old Testament prophets, 26
Modalism, 119
Monarchianism, 119
Moses, 54

Nebo, 144
Neo-orthodoxy, 102-6
Nicea, Council of, 14, 79, 92, 81-86, 97
Nicene Creed, 67, 81-96, 99, 100, 107, 111, 114
Niebuhr, Reinhold, 103

Origen, 80, 83
Osiris, 144
Otto, Rudolf, 105

Papias, bishop of Hierapolis, 44
Patrick, St., 155
Paul, 14, 24, 31-42, 58-64, 69, 73, 75, 76, 77-78, 79-80, 93, 114, 127
  his apocalyptic hope of Messiah, 24
  Christ seen as atoning sin-bearer, 40
  Christ seen as part of God, 38-39
  Hebraic influences, 48-49
  on the Incarnation, 71
  his inner conflicts, 28-30
  letters portray Jesus, 36-38
  his mental picture of Jesus, 33-34
  his mystical view of Jesus, 35
  his progress toward trinitarian creed, 41-42
  as a thinker, 39-40, 62-63
Pentecost, 23, 58, 71
Peter, 14, 25, 27, 36, 58, 71
  his apocalyptic hope of Messiah, 24
  confesses Christ at Caesarea Philippi, 21, 23-24
  preaches at Pentecost, 23

Philip, 58
Philo, 50, 65
Pittenger, W. Norman, *The Word Incarnate*, 91 n.
Platonists, 145
Prophets' hope for Messiah, 26
Psalms, son of God in, 70
Psychoanalysis, 30-31

Reid, James, 35-36
Resurrection, 22-23
Richardson, Cyril C., *The Doctrine of the Trinity*, 60-62, 86, 87, 130, 132, 142-43
Robertson, Frederick W., *Sermons on Bible Subjects*, 146
Robinson, John, 147
Roman Catholicism, 145-46
Roosevelt, Theodore, 143-44

Sabellianism, 144
Sabellius, 118, 119
Sangha, 144
Sargent, John Singer, 129-30
Saturninus, 75, 76
Saul, 54, 59
Sayers, Dorothy, *The Mind of the Maker*, 137, 138-40
Schweitzer, Albert, 111
Scott, Ernest F., *The Spirit in the New Testament*, 131
Shakespeare, 138
Shedd, William G. T., 116-17
Shekinah, 97
Shiva, 144
Simeon, 27
Simon Peter. *See* Peter
Socrates, 90
Son of God, 69-72; *see also* Jesus
Son of man, 49; *see also* Jesus
South, Dr. Robert, 120
Spirit. *See* Holy Spirit
Split personality, 30

Stephen, 32, 58
Stoicism, 112
Stoics, 50
Synoptic Gospels, 48, 55-57, 114

Taylor, Vincent, *The Person of Christ in New Testament Teaching*, 134
Temple, Archbishop William, *Readings in St. John's Gospel*, 44
Tersteegen, Gerhard, 120
Tertullian, 110-11, 115
Theodotus of Byzantium, 82
Thomas, George F., *The Christian Answer*, 85-86, 135, 150
Thornton, Lionel, *The Incarnate Lord*, 135
Tiberius, 77
Tillich, Paul, 13, 91, 92, 102
Titus, 73

Unitarians, 154 n.

Valentinus, 75, 76
Van Dusen, Henry Pitney, *Spirit, Son and Father*, 131-32, 143-44
Virgin birth, 18
Virgin, veneration of, 145-46
Vishnu, 144

Webb, C. C. J., 134
Welch, C., 134
Wesley, John, 36
Whale, J. S., 135
Williams, Daniel Day, *What Present Day Theologians Are Thinking*, 12-13
Word of God, 49-50, 65, 74, 145; *see also* Jesus
Wordsworth, 78

Zarpanitu, 144
Zechariah, 54-55